THE YAHOO;

A SATIRICAL RHAPSODY.

VELUTI IN SPECULUM.

"From what I have gathered from your own relation," said the king, "and the answers I have, with much pains, wringed and extorted from you, I can not but conclude the bulk of your natives to be the most pernicious race of little, odious vermin, that Nature ever suffered to crawl upon the surface of the earth."—*Gulliver's Travels.*

"My horror and astonishment are not to be described, when I observed in this abominable animal a perfect human figure."—*Ibid.*

"Where knaves and fools combined o'er all prevail."—*Byron.*

PREFACE

BY THE AMERICAN PUBLISHER.

This work first appeared in England, without name, perhaps because some of the allusions might be there considered personal, and libellous. It was republished, in parts, in *The Comet*, a periodical long since out of print. A few copies were also for sale in octavo form, decently bound, but at a high price. These also have disappeared; and if any remain, they will be sought after for the library, by those who wish to keep it in that form.

The object of the poem is to ridicule the vices and follies of mankind, especially those of pride, oppression, hypocrisy, or superstition; and its tendency is, consequently, to elevate society; while its merits as a poem, and its wit, are calculated to secure it a hearing, at the same time, the philosophy, the learning, and the information amassed in its notes, must afford solid food for those who profess to have no appetite for poetry.

Our object in reprinting it, is, not only to give it to the public, who are now deprived of it, but to give it in a cheap form, so that it may come within the reach of thousands who would otherwise never see it G. V.

PREAMBLE.

"O world! buzzard world! when wilt thou come out of thine infancy, and assume a beard, and a mind worthy of that beard! Learn to despise long coats; reject thy leaders and leading strings; stand upon thine own legs; be of age; look round thee, and distinguish truth and freedom from restraint and disguises.—*Dissertation upon Old Women.*

Thus apostrophized Thomas Gordon, a century ago; and can we pronounce the "Buzzard" to be much wiser at present, and in a condition to cast off its leading strings and long coats; or (to continue the metaphor) able to dispense with its go-cart and slavering-bib! That the world is very silly, considering its age, has been observed long since; which, however, is not much to be wondered at, when we recollect what great care is taken to perpetuate ignorance, and eradicate from the mind of youth every natural and rational idea, and to substitute in lieu the most nonsensical and stupifying metaphysical jargon, by which the mind becomes so contaminated,* that, under the name of religion, the horrible and cannibal idea of eating and drinking the "body and blood" of the deity they worship,† and to whom

* "Sa conception était d'autant plus vive et plus nette, que son enfance n'ayant point été chargée des inutilités et des sottises qui accablent la nôtre, les choses entraient dans sa cervelle sans nuage.—N'ayant rien appris dans son enfance, il n'avait point appris de prejugés. Son entendement n'ayant point été curbe par l'erreur était demeuré dans tout sa rectitude. Il voyait les choses comme elles sont, au lieu que les idées qu'on nous donne dans l'enfance nous les font voir toute notre vie comme elles ne sont point."—*L'Ingénu.*

† "And here we drink our Savior's blood."—*Watts' Hymns.* This is pretended to be only typical, &c.; but even when considered in that light, the bare idea is enough to put a Cherokee or a Hottentot to the blush, as the very quintessence of cannibalism.

they address their supplications, so far from exciting horror, is set down as the first and most important duty of a Christian YAHOO!

We now live in an *enlightened* age!—what a consoling and heart-warming consideration!—where the intellect is *spread* out like an apothecary's plaster, and the *mind marches* on with the strides of a Captain Bobadil, or Major Sturgeon; and every poor scribbler is sufficiently enlightened to know that if he wishes for pudding or praise, or is desirous of eating apple-tarts and cream with the maids of honor, or venison and custard with the lord-mayor, he must glide quietly on with the stream, and be careful how he hints, in the most remote manner, at the folly and vices of the Corinthian order.

The most distant allusion to their depravity will be deemed jacobinism; the slightest observations on the damning creed of Athanasius, blasphemy and atheism, and rational remarks on the so much admired fustian in heroics,* or cat-lap namby-pamby of "Peter and his Ass," will stamp him a low-lived Goth, and totally disqualify him for ever associating with the be-whiskered dandies and painted dolls in high life. All he could then expect would be the reward of the poor poet, as described by Pope—a garret with broken windows, and half a peck of coals; or to be admitted as a member of Foote's squad of scribblers, and start fair with them for a mess of milk porridge at breakfast time.

Reading Public (to adopt the fashionable slang, but who seem to read to little purpose), ten thousand pens are worn and wearing to the stumps, working day and night in pro-

* See the "Ode on the Battle of Waterloo," where Carnage is "God's daughter," among other instances of the sublime and beautiful; and poor Peter's donkey's brotherly three groans, in the slop-dawdle way; with "Betty Foy," the "toothless mastiff bitch," &c., &c., all of which, after being properly daubed over by *learned* and *impartial* reviewers, were purchased with avidity by an *intelligent* reading public, to their great edification and delight.

A lady, who was purchasing a collection of books, asked Dr. Johnson whether she should be guided in the selection by the reviews. "By all means, madam," replied the doctor; "they will serve you as an infallible guide; purchase all that they revile, but none that they praise, and you will be sure to be right."—*Colton's Hypocrisy*

curing wherewithal to glut thy insatiate and ravenous maw,* and, with a very few exceptions, with the same sort of mawkish stuff; one scribbler following another in the same dull beaten track, like horses in a team, as Parson Hickeringill observes† — "one's nose in t'other's tail," all singing to the same tune; the parrot-like gabble, and the cuckoo's dull note; everlastingly bellowing forth in praise of the "powers that be;" blarneying with fulsome panegyric the "best of kings;"‡ an illustrious nobility;§ the pure and sapient Collective;‖ the glorious Constitution; with the never-enough-to-be-praised British nation, as pre-

* "The many-headed beast is a foul feeder," says Dr. Southey; and the doctor is very right, as appears by its feeding on such filthy food as Lot and his daughters; 'Zekel's *buttered bun;* and the two Brims, whose "teats of virginity were bruised," &c. (Ezekiel xxxiii.) besides gorging every Lord's day on the *bloody sweat* of the Lamb.

Now let us suppose a Lord Fopdoodle, or a Sir Dilberry Diddle, who had hurried to be in time at a grand dinner party of Corinthians of the highest class, should arrive in a state of perspiration, wiping his phiz, and exclaiming that he was in a "bloody sweat," what a consternation and turning up of eyes it would occasion, with the stamp of downright blackguard on his character for ever after.

† "Pillars of Priestcraft."

‡ Yes! and as wise as good!—See P. Pindar's account of the *royal* dead mutton sent to Fleet market for sale; and of the more than Paul Pry curiosity to discover the seam in the apple-dumpling; with other Solomon-like specimens of profound sagacity, in the late money scraping, church-going SHEEPYO AMERICANUS.

§ Titles were offered to the leading members of Congress, as a lure, during the American war; in answer to which Dr. Franklin replied —"Peerages! Alas, sir! our long observation of the vast servile majority of your peers voting constantly for every measure proposed by a minister, however weak or wicked, leaves us little respect for them."—*Franklin's Correspondence.*

‖ A parliament of knaves and sots,
(Members by name you must not mention),
He keeps in pay, and buys their votes,
With here a place, and there a pension.
Lord Rochester.

"You will receive herewith," says Frederick II., in a letter to D'Alembert, during the American war, "the remedy which you request for the hydrophobia, or bite of mad dogs. The medicine has performed wonderful cures, and I would recommend that it be sent to the English Parliament. Its members act like a legion of lunatics." —*Belsham's History of England.*

eminent in virtue, courage, humanity,* charity, and every other good quality: every third page of their luminous productions larded (like a round of beef with gobbets of fat bacon) with "the Lord's goodness," the "blessing of Heaven, Divine Providence, a precious Redeemer, the Most High," &c , &c., not forgetting the "inestimable treasure of the Holy Scriptures, which excelleth all the treasures of the earth" (as the translators of the Jew book told the *brutish* Solomon in their dedication), with other fear-the-lord gibberish, of a similar quality.

* *British* Humanity is the eternal cry with which we are deafened; and, indeed, whenever a subscription has been set on foot for the poor *Dutch*, poor *Swiss*, distressed *Germans*, or other foreigners, with a recommendation from royalty, a considerable sum has always been raised; but when four or five hundred poor creatures, their own dear Britons, were cut to pieces, and trampled under the iron hoofs of horses, indiscriminately, men, women, and children, by infuriated, half-drunken savages, who had their sabres sharpened expressly for the butchery, and the distress and horror it might have been supposed would have excited general compassion among a people self-styled the very quintessence of humanity, and the *true Christian* milk of human kindness; but no! a yell of barbarous exultation was set up; and a cry of "served 'em right," was heard from Cornwall to the Orkney islands, among the *genteel* classes of toad-eaters and lick-spittles, in consequence of the bloodhounds receiving the thanks of the king for their heroic exploits.* A subscription was set on foot for the relief of such as survived, as well as for the widows and orphans of the murdered, and a few hundred pounds raised, principally by the "swinish multitude," in their clubs and societies; as it was considered disgraceful in the *quality* line to contribute! Talk of British humanity! What compassion was shown toward poor Byrne, who was imprisoned and cruelly whipped, for accusing (and justly) a stinking beast of a bishop of an unnatural crime; and who, afterward, when detected, got *off*, having a snivelling lord for his brother, as well as the interest of the Church, who do not like *such* affairs to be brought to light before the daddies of the lord. Humanity!! Who ever interfered in behalf of Mrs. and Miss Carlile, and Mrs. Wright, while suffering in loathsome prisons, for their integrity and virtuous advocacy of truth? Who commiserated the dreadful state of the unfortunate Ogden, when expiring in jail under the torments of a rupture? Did not the spouting cock of the walk set the whole kennel of collectives in a roar of laughter, by adverting to the sufferings of the "*revered* and *ruptured*" Ogden?—Humanity! Pshaw! Twaddle! Fudge! Old Nick is humane to his favorite imps, no doubt.

* This horrible tragedy, commonly called the Manchester massacre, which was promoted and directed by two parsons, was discussed in the upper kennel (house of lords), when 150 most noble lords voted their approbation.

"Whatever is, is right," is the cry of the kennel, consequently there can be nothing wrong; and when a convict swings off in fine style from the new drop, are they not assured by the Rev. Mr. Diddleum, that after they have repented of their sins, and received absolution, they will mount up to the regions of bliss, be welcomed by the angelic host, and occasion great rejoicing in heaven?* Does not this prove incontestably that "all is for the best," and that "whatever is, is right?"

"The man whose soul the blackest vices taint,
For heaven's *glory* makes a damned good saint."
Peter Pindar.

"Repent then all ye rogues, ye'll be forgiven,
And give the saints a holiday in heaven."

And surely we must acknowledge this to be a most consoling, as well as an encouraging doctrine for thieves and cut-throats, who ought to felicitate themselves on being the humble instruments of so much merry-making, when they are dismissed by John Ketch, Esq., with a hempen collar of their order round their necks, as a passport for kingdom-come, of which no doubt they are not a little proud upon their arrival, and swagger away like evangelicals of the first water.† Let us, therefore, sing to the praise of the Lamb, and his head-spouter Paul, and the blessed doctrine of "justification by faith, and atonement for sin," so admirably calculated for the spread of wickedness, and the knowledge-box of the intelligent Yahoo!‡

* "I say unto you, that joy shall be in heaven over one sinner that repenteth, more than over ninety and nine just persons which need no repentance."—Luke xv.

† It is a common saying among felons, that, "when the worst comes to the worst, they can tip the devil a *Redesdale*, and get white-washed by the parson at the gallows."

‡ "To make the entrance sure for rogue or thief,
As well as him who lives by honest means,
Our hero so arranged his belief,
That even the rogue, provided that he gains
Both faith and grace, shonld stand the better chance,
As all his previous sins would but enhance

"His worth in heaven; at least we're often told,
That o'er repentant sinners by the saints

But although "all is for the best," and everything under the superintendence of Divine Providence, without whose permission a sparrow cannot fall to the ground (as the spiritual Jack in a box assures his assinine audience at the Fudge-office), yet so little reliance is placed on the assertion by the poor bewildered Yahoo, that he is incessantly worrying the great Jehovah to change his immutable decrees to gratify some selfish or ridiculous whim, notwithstanding his drawling whine of "thy will be done." One asks for an east wind, while another wants a west, &c.—And when we consider that the Turks are all bawling and screaming on Friday, the Jews groaning and grunting on Saturday, and the Christians snivelling and psalm-singing on Sunday; and that, in the intermediate days, the Esquimaux, Catabaws, Winnebagoes, Otaheitans, Hottentots, &c., are all *hard at it*, howling and bellowing out Divine *service* in their way, one can not help thinking that the situation of the great Jehovah, so far from being desirable, would not be accepted of in exchange by his dark-skinned antagonist in the cellar, provided he was obliged to continue superintendent of the two-legged grubs called Yahoos; and, that the latter has the least harassing and unpleasant employment of the two, especially as he can take an airing when he pleases, and even trot up stairs on levée days, strutting about like a crow in a gutter, and gossipping with the great Jehovah "en famille."—Job i.

Those "whom the Lord loveth he chastiseth," we are told, "and scourgeth every son whom he receiveth;" therefore the more we are drubbed the more thankful we ought to be, and the more convinced of his loving-kindness; but, unfortunately, we are sometimes at a loss to ascertain whether it is by the rod of the Lord, or by that of the Devil, the stripes are inflicted, as the latter was permitted to give poor Job, who was an "upright man and feared the Lord," a confounded whacking;* so that it seems the Lord punish-

"There is more joy, by near an hundred fold,
Than o'er the virtuous souls, of whom complaints
Had never reached the gods:—this was a bribe,
A fine inducement for the sinning tribe!" *Prize Poem on St. Paul.*

* Poor Job! he might well lament that he "came out of the belly."—Job. iii.

es us for our wickedness, and the devil for our good qualities! Bravo! This is being between anvil and hammer with a vengeance! But if all's for the best, and everything right, why should we grumble? If we are to be bundled into hell, let us eat our pudding, and hold our tongues, and make the best of a bad bargain; it's all what pleases the Lord, or it would not be, and we ought to thank God for everything—as an old woman used to be continually telling her unlucky cub of a grandson, who one day came running in crying, "Don't you say we should thank God for everything, granny?"—"Yes, to be sure, my dear," says she. "Well then," says Dick, "I've tumbled down with the basket of eggs you bid me carry to Goody Grump, and they're all smashed."—"You unlucky brat," cries poor granny, "I've a good mind to lug your ears."—"Why, I thought," cries Dick, "we were to thank God for everything; but that's not all, for our cow's dead, and is lying on the common; so there's something else to thank God for, besides the broken eggs, granny."

"To live in society," says an intelligent writer, "we must sympathize with it; but no sympathy can subsist between the knaves and fools, who are playing the game of 'make-believe,' and quarrelling over the stakes, and the person who sees through their trickery, and despises its objects. There is no disguising from the cool eye of philosophy, that all living creatures exist in a state of natural warfare; and that man (in hostility with all) is at enmity also with his own species—man is the natural enemy of man; and society, unable to change his nature, succeeds but in establishing a hollow truce, by which fraud is substituted for violence. The honestest and the boldest man must hide a good half of his thoughts, if he would not be lodged between four walls, or interdicted *ab aqua et igni*. He who has not the courage to encounter a mass of evil, must pass through life with a bridle perpetually on his tongue. He must hear with a becoming gravity the words honor and patriotism proceeding from the lips of pollution—he must hold law to be synonymous with justice, persecution with tolerance, general pauperism with national prosperity, priestcraft with piety, and plunder with loyalty and religion."

Hobbes affirms the state of nature to be a state of war;

and in what does that of civilized life differ, except that it is carried on under a masked battery? One Yahoo will always covet the luxuries and superfluities of another, of which he is himself destitute (whatever he may pretend to the contrary) in spite of the interdictions of Porteusian bibles,* or canting tracts of "Christ and a Crust," &c., with which he is gutted till the gorge rises, and but to little purpose.† Commandments from the Decalogue may be solemnly mouthed out by the priest, forbidding the Yahoo to covet his neighbor's goods, and children told that they must not hanker after the cherries or toys of their playfellows; all which are as scrupulously attended to, and with as much effect as proclamations would be by hungry mastiffs, forbidding them to covet each other's horse-flesh. And is not the same selfish or envious disposition shown even in factitious wants; one Yahoo of the higher class, will envy another who has obtained permission from the master of the puppet-show, to paint a fool's bauble on the pannels of his booby-hutch, or stitch it on the corner of his mucus wrappers and scullion's dishclouts, to which he thinks he has a better pretension himself.

* The Yahoo, it seems, is now ashamed of the filthy language of his *holy* bible, which is at present filtering through ecclesiastical strainers to clarify it for the Godly! This is at least an indication of a *spread.* But is it not to be lamented that the emasculated parts, or luscious exuberances of the Holy Scripture (to say nothing of the castration of Gibbon and Shakspere), should thus be lost? Would it not be advisable to collect and publish them under the title of, "*Tit-Bits for Godly Gormandizers,*" as a kind of spiritual Lamb's fry? (we now can furnish a penny list for selection) for the benefit of delicate ladies, who might thus learn, among other holy matters, on what account admission was refused to the "congregation of the Lord."—Deuter. xxiii. The time is undoubtedly approaching when this nauseons and disgusting book will be carefully excluded from every decent family; in spite of the parsons, who are working night and day, like devils upon a mud wall, to support it. That such demoralizing trash should be considered as essential to the poor Yahoo's salvation, affords a decided proof of the superiority of his intellect, so much boasted of!

† The report of the committee for inquiring into the cause of the increase of commitments and convictions in London and Middlesex, states, that notwithstanding all we hear of schools, and the progress of education, juvenile depravity was never so unlimited in degree, or so deperate in character.—*Southey's Colloquies.*

"All envy power in others, and complain
Of that which they would perish to obtain.—*Churchill.*"

And, as was observed by Sir Robert Walpole, that by obliging one friend, he was certain to create a dozen enemies. Such is the loving-kindness of Christian Yahoos to each other, though taught to love their neighbors as themselves! but they are all tarred with the same brush, and play the same game in their turn.

Some author has observed, that it is to be lamented, the great Jehovah, after proving the incorrigibility of the Yahoo race, by sousing them all (with the exception of eight, whose offspring proved no better), like so many puppies in a horse-pond, and smiting, and "swearing in his wrath," did not create a fresh batch, free from the defects of their Adamite progenitors,* instead of sending his only *begotten Son* as a sacrifice, in company with a ghost (one to milk a ram and the other to hold the pail), and all for what? *Cui bono?* for although the said ghost fills the paunch, or the sconce, no matter which, of every reverend prig to this very day, and without doubt inspires him to sputter forth his Godly jabber;† the poor Yahoos remain lost muttons, and continue to be trundled wholesale and retail into the tithe-barn of the OLD ONE.

But is it not very extraordinary and inconceivable, that the only begotten Son, aided by the ghost, and under the guidance or superintendence of the Father, in their soul-saving mission, sent expressly to take away the sins of the world, should have succeeded no better? Three to one,

* Much crime and misery would have been avoided in this "best of all possible worlds," if the great Jehovah, when he *dabbed* up the Yahoo, had clapped a bell or clicker within him, which should have given the alarm whenever he told a lie. There would then have been but little want of law and gospel.

† This ghost, it appears, first exhibited himself "as the sound of a mighty rushing wind"—an odd way for a ghost!—and settled in the shape of "fiery cloven tongues" on the jobbernols of a set of lazy lubbers, who, instead of minding their fishing-tackle and leather-dressing, went about the highways *Mawworming*. But, how do the parsons of the present day contrive to get so full of this ghost, by whom they affirm they are called on to spout? We see no "fiery tongues" on their lumber-garrets, though we hear them from their mouths denouncing hell-fire to all unbelievers, and such as dare to pry into their holy pilfering mysteries.

they say, are odds at foot-ball; and who could suppose in such a contest they would come off second best, and leave the grim fiend triumphant, to snap his black fingers, and laugh at their ineffectual efforts to rescue the Yahoo from his clutches (which they themselves admit, and to continue in his career, "Going about like a roaring lion" [oh, that it were a Picadilly one, that we might laugh at its braying!], and seeking whom he may devour.

But "why Goramity no kill debil?" as Friday said to his master, "Goramity all good, all strong!" Ah, why, in deed! poor Crusoe was sadly puzzled, and wished he had a bishop at his elbow to answer the poor ignorant savage. Whence has the ugly rascal so much power? Is it not astonishing, after the repeated attempts of the *Lamb* & Co. (Goramity's delegates here on earth), to rescue the poor Yahoo from debil's claws, by bugaboo visitations, bible-poring, tract-snuffling, and hymn-singing,* as well as by catechizing, churching, confirming, and *parsonizing* in every way possible, that he should still continue in a state of sin? Is it with filthy lucre and the "mammon of unrighteousness" that Satan lures the precious soul of the Yahoo from the *narrow* to the *broad* way, which leadeth to the bottomless pit? Yea, verily it looketh very like it, for *that* the Wicked One knoweth full well to be a never-failing bait, and holdeth it up before the peepers of such as are not strong in the *Lord Jesus;* even as the recruiting sergeant holdeth up a *shiner* to tempt the bumpkin to cast aside his smock-frock, and become a gentleman. And when do our spiritual pastors and masters, who are eternally croaking about

* The following is a specimen of the Godly cat-lap the saints regale the Lord with in their gospel shops:—

"What is now to children the dearest thing here?
To be the *Lamb's* lambkins, and chickens most dear.
Such lambkins are nourished with food that is best;
Such chickens sit safely and warm in their nest.
And when Satan at an hour,
Comes our chickens to devour,
Let the children's angel say,
These are Christ's chicks, go thy way."

Southey's Life of Wesley.

See more of this stuff in the Bath Guide, p. 57; with an excellent parody, p. 129.

the depravity of the heart, and the corruptive quality of riches, ever renounce them if they are possibly come-at-able? "Tant que la fortune, les honneurs, et le *vice* seront d'un cote, la pauvreté, l'abandon, et la *vertu* de l'autre, le choix des hommes ne sera pas douteux. On pourra vivre dans le vice, sans vivre dans l'opprobre, on pourra meme se perdre pour une bonne action: mais il y aura un culte public, et ce culte fleurira au milieu des mauvaises mœurs, comme un plante parasite sur un tronc pourri."‡

"If our tongues correspond with our hearts," says Dean Swift, "men will avoid our company, because their faults will not be complimented; and if the heart and tongue do not agree, we must certainly have a very mean opinion of ourselves, if we have the least notion of honesty; nevertheless it is so necessary in life, that it has become an *art*. He that can make his countenance applaud an object, though his heart despises it, is what is called a *well-bred* man, a polite gentleman, and *one* who knows the world."

The following *petite ouvrage* was composed at different times, from observations of the prevailing follies and vices, and irrational conduct of the lords of reason; the greatest part many years since, as may be supposed by the allusion to Master Betty, the Cock Lane ghost, &c. It was not intended for the press, but written merely as a matter of amusement, in a profound retirement, far from the metropolis, and is now brought by accident before the reading public for their recreation in this "march of mind," and "spread of intellect" era; not with any view to profit, as may readily be imagined, but rather in the full persuasion that by ninety-nine out of every hundred of the enlightened and intelligent Yahoo race, the author will be consigned to the fiery lake of the Black Prince. This must naturally be expected: very few are pleased when their vices and absurdities are held up to derision; especially their darling superstitious practices of hocus-pocus, mumbo-jumbo, and fee-faw-fum; that being by church logic a "sin against the Holy Ghost," and never to be forgiven. The *Odium Theologicum*, which, as Mr. Lawrence justly observes, is the

* Letter from the Marquis de Rivarol to M. Necker.

"most concentrated essence of rancor and animosity," is sure to be vomited forth against all such productions as militate against their usurpations, and expose their mountebank jugglery; for the same reason that policemen are execrated and fired at by a banditti of thieves when molested in the exercise of *their* profession. This indeed is not to be wondered at, agreeing with *Square's* "rule of right and fitness of things." Caw me, caw thee, and *vice versa*, curry me, curry thee.

But there is another tribe whose malevolence is conspicuous upon such occasions, who are paid, as well as the former class, for the venom they spit forth, and whose slander and scurrility is directed against every one whose principles are suspected of being inimical to the "powers that be," whether of the Lord Jesus or of the Lord of Hell, who, as, Lord Byron observes, "feed by lying and slandering and slake their thirst by evil speaking," who skulk in the dark, and like a hydra, or many-headed monster, begin hissing and barking at those who express disapprobation of the follies and vices of the higher orders, many of whom are notorious for their apostacy, and obtain laureateships, and monuments in cathedrals,* from their direliction of truth

The great *Moralist*, or *Rex porcorum*, it was confidently reported, during the American war, and soon after he "changed his coat, and would have changed his skin" (as Lord Byron says of the laureate), was engaged in drawing up inflammatory addresses to the negroes in the Southern states, instigating them to set fire to their master's plantations, and go over to the British army, where they would be protected and rewarded! At that time Edmund Burke, one of the chiefs in the gang of apostates, was such a violent enemy to royalty, that he proposed in the collective a reduction of the kingly power, even in the article of guttling! And in later days, have we not *Wat Tyler* staring us in the face, among other barefaced instances of *sop-in-the-pan* hunters! who have totally disregarded character and principle? But

"The silver turnip's tempting skin,
Draws such base hogs through thick and thin."

Or, as Churchill observes,

"Convinced, I changed (can any man do more?
And have not greater patriots changed before?);
Changed, I at once (can any man do less?),
Without a single blush, that change confess;
Confess it with a manly kind of pride,
And quit the losing for the winning side."

and principle;* possessing supple "*wha wants me*" sort of consciences, and who are ready for any dirty work at the nod of their employers: such have hissed and barked at Gibbon, Dr. Wolcot, Horace Walpole, Lady Morgan, Lord Byron, and other writers of distinguished abilities; but they are paid for their work, and it's all one to such hirelings whether they labor in the Lord's vineyard or the devil's.

That we live in a vitiated age (notwithstanding the so much boasted "spread and stream of intellect"), and that a general corruption has taken place, and rendered morals a laughing-stock, is notorious and universally admitted; but then we are blessed with a superabundance of godliness, alias cant,† to qualify it and make amends: every pious swindler now can let off half a dozen gospel squibs in your face, about Paul's snipping off a bit of poor Tim's trapstick,‡ and such holy stuff, and give you chapter and verse, like Cuddy's mother in the "Tales of my Landlord," while he is drawing the watch or handkerchief out of your pocket.

"Such is the modern *apostolic* race,
Reformed, regenerated rogues of *grace*—
Who sigh for heaven, yet God in *Mammon* see,
And pick a pocket on the suppliant knee;
One eye to God, lamenting moral evil,
The other winking down upon the devil:
One voice to Heaven, 'To good my heart incline!'
And one in whispers, 'Satan, I am thine!'"

Peter Pindar.

And to the same tune singeth Nic,§ "Non vi e bisogna che tu abbia tutte le qualita, che ho detto [religion] ma solamente che tu *mostri* di averle." And again, in speaking

* "Oh, for a world, in principle as chaste
As this is gross and selfish; over which
Custom and prejudice shall bear no sway,
That govern all things here, should'ring aside
The meek and modest truth, and forcing her
To seek a refuge from the tongue of strife
In nooks obscure, far from the ways of men."—*Cowper.*

† It is rather remarkable that all official ecclesiastical documents, hatched and cuddled into shape at Lambeth, should be signed by the grand humbug, CANT! It is a curious coincidence, and certainly very appropriate.

‡ Acts of the Apostles, xvi.

§ Machiavelli.

on the same topic, he observes, "Ma quest'ultima qualità e quella che importa *piu di ogni altra* di avere *esteriormente!*" This is instruction for a prince! Cant and kingdom come, for ever! Amen.

The Yahoo race consists of two classes, the bamboozlers and the bamboozled; the cry of the latter (of the lowest class) is "GIN and JESUS," while that of the upper class is "CHURCH and STATE," with a "let well alone." The motto of the knowing ones is, "Si populus vult decipi decipiatur;" i. e.,

"If humbugged thus the people choose to be,
Why, let 'em, since it brings the chink to me
There's none so blind as those who will not see."

"Oh, Dio mio!" said a recent pope, after giving the apostolical blessing to fifty or sixty thousand persons from the balcony of St. Peter's church on Easter Sunday, the troops gaping to receive it, and the multitude all on their marrow-bones, the cannons roaring and bells jingling, "Oh, Dio mio! quanto e facile di coglionare le gente!"*

The mob who stand gaping at the cup and ball juggler, are as much delighted as Mr. Lickpenny, who pockets their contributions; as Hudibras observes—

"Doubtless the pleasure is as great
In being cheated as to cheat."

READING PUBLIC, shouldst thou relish the above preamble, *en avant*, there's more sour krout for thee, and BUON PRO VI FACCIA.

* Forsyth's Travels.

AUTHORITIES.

"For that which befalleth the sons of men befalleth beasts, even one thing befalleth them, as the one dieth so dieth the other; yea, they have all one breath, so that a man hath no pre-eminence above a beast; all go unto one place; all are of the dust, and all turn to dust again."—Eccles. iii.

"For the dead know not anything, neither have they any more a reward."—Ibid. ix.

"Nevertheless, man being in honor, abideth not; he is like the beasts that perish."—Psalm xlix.

"So he that goeth down to the grave shall come up no more. He shall return no more to his house."—Job ix.

'So man lieth down and riseth not till the heavens be no more, they shall not awake, nor be raised out of their sleep."—Job xiv.

"He shall perish for ever like his own dung."—Ibid xx.

"We are all as an unclean thing."*—Isaiah lxiv.

"What is man that he should be clean? how much more abominable and filthy is man?"—Job xv.

"For the imagination of man's heart is evil from his youth."—Gen. viii.

"The heart of man is deceitful above all things and desperately wicked."—Jesus.

"Why died I not from the womb? why did I not give up the ghost when I came out of the belly? For now should I have lain still and been quiet; I should have slept; then had I been at rest."—Job iii.

"Understand, ye brutish among the people; and ye fools, when will ye be wise?"—Psalm xciv.†

"Every man is brutish by his own knowledge."—Jeremiah li.

* What that is may be found out in Deuteronomy xxiii.

† Never while they read bibles.

THE YAHOO.

"De tous les animaux qui s'elèvent dans l'air,
Qui marchent sur la terre, ou nagent dans la mer,
De Paris au Pérou, du Japon jusqu' à Rome,
Le plus sot animal, à mon avis, c'est l' homme."—*Boileau.*

"Could I but choose what flesh and blood I'd wear,
I'd be a dog, a monkey, or a bear;
Or anything but that vain animal,
Who is so proud of being rational."—*Lord Rochester.*

So sung Boileau, when Louis, styled the Great,
Kept up his court of profligates in state:
So Wilmot sung in Charles's vicious reign;*
And is there now less reason to complain?
The race is much improved we're told—'tis true;
It is improved—in vice, and folly too:†
From bad to worse, whatever is pretended,
As ale that's sour in sultry weather's mended.
The present "all-accomplished" YAHOO breed,
May boast their "spread of intellect," indeed:
The "best of education" now's the word
From tripe and dog's-meat venders, to my lord:
But does this *lacker* change the YAHOO's nature?‡

* "His court, the dissolute and hateful school
Of wantonness, where vice was taught by rule."—*Cowper.*

† "Such now are held as nothing.—We begin
Where our sires ended, and improve in sin;
Rack our invention, and leave nothing new
In vice and folly for our sons to do."—*Churchill.*

‡ "The boasted knowledge of England," says a certain apostat "has not sunk deep; it is like the golden surface of a *lackered* watc which covers, and but barely covers, the base metal. The great ma

Is he not still the same vile, silly creature?
The "spread of intellect," so much his boast,
Is but leaf-gold spread on a rotten post.
Polish'd he may be, varnished high enough,
But still 'tis ornament on paltry stuff.
Can a Sir-rev. . . . be fragrant made
By stirring it about with marmalade?
"Then just as much you'll mend the breed," says Quin,
To Jerry Melford, with malicious grin.*
But what says Swift?—"Oh, dear!" Miss Dawdle cries,
"That filthy parson's writings I despise;
Such poor, low, vulgar stuff, is never read
By quality, or such as are well bred."†
Your pardon, Ma'am, a few lines from the Dean,
Multum in parvo, tells you what we mean.

Swift tells us then, a cook once tried to make
A certain something into a plum-cake;
He mixed it up with eggs, and plums and spice,
And candied orange-peel, to make it nice;

of the people are as ignorant, and as well contented with their ignorance, as any of the most illiterate nations in Europe; and even among those who might be expected to know better, it is astonishing how slowly information makes way to any practical utility."—*Letters from Spain.*

* "But when I appealed to Quin, and asked him, if he did not think such an unreserved mixture (of the higher classes with the lower at Bath) would improve the whole mass?—'Yes,' said he, 'as a plate of marmalade would improve a pan of Sir-rev . . . . ce.'"—*Humphrey Clinker.*

† The works of Swift, Smollett, Fielding, Gay, and even Pope, in consequence of the vast "spread of intellect," are at present considered as low and vulgar, and unfit for the perusal of persons *genteelly* brought up, as it is termed, who by everlasting poring over the novelties of the day, larded with "dove-like eyes, long silken eye-lashes, graceful attitudes, sylph-like forms, exquisitely fine-formed limbs, graceful bendings over and sweeping the strings of the harp," &c., &c., have become so highly-purified and double-refined in their feelings, that they are almost frightened into fits by any expression of humor. Lord Byron is now scouted, it seems, in what is termed *genteel* society. "Plus les mœurs sont dépravés," says Voltaire, with great truth, "plus les expressions deviennent mesurées, on croit regagner en langage ce qu'on a perdu en vertu. La pudeur s'est enfuite des cœurs et s'est refugiée sur les lèvres."

Then sugared it all o'er to make it sweet,
But still he found it wasn't fit to eat;
At last, "God rot the nasty mess!" he muttered,
"It isn't worth a fig when cooked and buttered;
To mix good things with bad, wiseacres say,
Is only throwing your good things away."

Thus, tho' the best of education's given,
There still predominates the native leaven.
One might define the present polished race,
An outside virtuous, with an inside base;
Or classed with quadrupeds, a kind of monkeys,
Or orang-outangs, crossed with wolves and donkeys; *
Whose varied actions analyzed, disclose
The hateful nature both of these and those.†
The gods, we're told, produced the precious crew
To laugh at, when they knew not what to do;
When they were all *ennui'd* with state affairs,
To make them merry they would peep down stairs:
And sure the tom-fool's actions here on earth,
Must cause their godships everlasting mirth.

Who would suppose, to hear him boast his shade,
Man bore so great resemblance to an ape?‡

* "Read hist'ry thro', in every page
You'll see how men with thoughtless rage,
Each other rob, destroy, and burn,
To serve a priest's or statesman's turn;
Tho' acting in a diff'rent name,
Yet always ASSES, much the same."—*Dodsley.*

† "Our race in general," says Horace Walpole, "is pestilently bad and malevolent;" and Lord Byron seems of the same opinion, since he observes, "that mankind are every way despicable in their different absurdities."—*Letters to Dallas.*

‡ "Of beasts, it is confessed, the ape
Comes nearest us in human shape:
Like man he imitates each fashion,
And malice is his ruling passion."—*Goldsmith.*

"C'est une grande question parmi les Nègres," says Voltaire, "s'ils sont descendus des singes, ou si les singes sont venus d'eux. Nos sages ont dit que l'homme est l'image de Dieu! Voilà une plaisante image de l'Etre éternel! qu'un nez noir épaté, avec peu ou point d'intelligence."—*Lettres D'Amabed.*

The monkey's form is ugly, he'll confess;
But what's his own, when undisguised by dress?
Of *elegant* baboons he does not talk,*
Because they do not on their *hind* legs walk;†
But give me pug; what puppy, tho' from France,
Can vie with him in gambol, or in dance?‡
If you the monkey with the man compare,
You'll own the latter dances like a bear.
Pug has beside a comfortable coat,
But what's the Yahoo's hide worth? not a groat.§
To judge between them fairly, he should strip,
And show how much he owes to brother Snip.
If he (as to compare he should) appeared
In buff, and with a hideous shaggy beard;‖
With tangled locks, soot-colored, we'll suppose,
Thro' which you just could spy his eyes and nose;

* This epithet (elegant) is now applied to every whiskered puppy who struts up and down Pall-Mall, or in the Park, with a cockade in his hat, by the wishy-washy, cat-lap novel-writers of the day, who are, it is true, mostly of the feminine gender, and therefore more excusable.

† "Quelques philosophes ont defini l'homme un singe qui rit, d'autres un animal crédule. Cet animal, ajoutent-ils, est monté sur deux jambes, a les doigts flexible, des mains adroites: il a beaucoup de besoins, en consequence beaucoup d'industrie. D'ailleurs aussi vain et aussi orgueilleux que crédule: il pense que le monde est fait pour lui." —*Helvetius.*

‡ "What mortal can like monkeys dance a jig?
What man from bough to bough like jackoo springs?
Ingenious rogue, who twists his tail and swings."—*Pindar.*

§ John Ziska, it is said, desired that after his death a drum might be made of his skin, which he predicted when beat would always terrify his enemies, and occasion them to fly. "Que le succes," says Helvetius, "justifia toujours;" consequently the *Yahoo's* hide is good for something.

‖ As God the Father is always represented with a majestic beard, and has made man in his own image, it may be fairly presumed Adam was furnished with this superb ornament to the human phiz. Is it not then in the spirit of contumacy that the Yahoo deprives himself of it, upon the supposition that he looks better without it? At least, this was the opinion of the old twattlers, called "Fathers of the Church." Tertullian observes, "Shaving the beard is a lie against our own faces, and an impious attempt to improve the works of the Creator."—*Gibbon,* chap. xv.

Uncombed, unwashed, unlicked, as he was first
When he was manufactured out of dust;
There's not a creature that has any sense,
But what would give poor pug the preference;
Instead of viewing him with fond delight,
They'd run as from the devil, in a fright;
Yet this conceited, silly, blown-up elf,
Affirms Jehovah's made just like himself.*
Formed like his Maker! who could then suppose,
To hide the workmanship he'd want small-clothes?†
Made like a God! in great Jehovah's shape!
Yes, so he would be, tho' he were an ape.
If monkeys e'er made gods, their *noble* natures
Would make them like themselves, with *handsome* features;
See *godlike* YAHOOS their devotions pay
In Cloacina's temple, night and day:
The rich, the poor, the humble, and the great,
Set in fine attitudes, and—grunt in state.‡
Like other *noble* animals, we find
He eats, and sleeps, and propagates his kind:
But then to propagate's so like a beast—
For Yahoo's in Jehovah's form, at least:§

* "If God has made man in his own image," says Helvetius, "the biped has returned the compliment by making God in *his*;" or, as Voltaire observes:—

"C'est que l'homme amoureux de son sot esclavage,
Fit dans son prejuge Dieu même en son image
Nous l'avons fait injuste, emporté, vain, jaloux,
Séducteur, inconstant, barbare comme nous."

† *Small-clothes* and *inexpressibles* are the delicate molly-coddle terms of the dandified, cravat-tying puppies of the present day; to whom the very sound of the word breeches would inevitably occasion fainting fits, and require an application of the smelling-bottle for their recovery.

‡ See an illustrative print called the "State of the Nation," published by Bowles & Co., St. Paul's Church Yard, in which half a dozen "lords of the creation," and as many ladies, are exhibited in grand style, pouring out their tributary offerings at the shrine of the goddess.

§ It is very extraordinary that the action of reproduction of such a *noble* animal as a *Yahoo*, to which the great Jehovah himself contributes, by furnishing it with a SOUL, should be considered as shameful and wicked (from the sinful lusts of the flesh), while the destruction of thousands of the *noble* race is highly honorable and even

And tho' God says, "increase and multiply,"
About the business they seem rather shy;
Their females eagerly at times they seek,
And then in some dark corner with them sneak.*
Indeed to eat, to drink, to sleep, to propagate,
Degrades God's "images" at any rate;†
And with their pride and boasting but ill suits,
As on a level placing them with brutes.
Made like a god! what! do they then suppose
Their god has, like themselves, mouth, eyes, and nose?
The bloated biped, arrogant and blind,
Has SEX and FORM to Nature's God assigned!
(With bushy beard and genitals, no doubt,
How could he ever get a son without?)
Of gender masculine their god must be,
And in large letters written HIM and HE?‡
Sitting in clouds upon a golden throne,
In company with Holy Ghost and Son;
While twenty thousand trumpeters sit round him,
Whose blasts must now and then confound him:
Such heaven, without a mistress or a wife,
Must be a stupid, muddling sort of life,
Oh, what a DEITY! give me old Jove,
With all his jolly company above;

glorious!—Bolingbroke observes, that "from an excess of pride man avoids everything that assimilates him to the brute, and consequently gets out of sight for the business of procreation, as well as in some other humiliating actions by which his dignity is lowered, and which places him on the same level with the quadruped."—See *Philosophical Essays*, vol. i., p. 7, and vol. iv., p. 126.

* "None shun the day and seek the shades of night,
But those whose actions can not bear the light."—*Churchill.*

† "Lorsqu'on voit," says Montaign, "un chancelier avec sa simarre, sa large péruke, et son air compose, il n'est point de tableau plus plaisant à se faire, que de se peindre ce même chancelier sur la chaise-percee, ou consommant l'œuvre de marriage."

‡ in the present rage of fanatical cant, these pronouns are always written in large and marked characters, in the trashy productions with which we are inundated; but a N. B. should be added, to instruct the reader to turn up his eyes to the ceiling, and also to cross himself (as a Methodist does at the mention of the devil), whenever these representatives of the great Jehovah stare him in the face.

And not this gloomy being, with his clerk,
To watch what Yahoos do when in the dark;*
And write down whether they all fast and pray,
Or eat a sprat on such and such a day.
If to your maker *gender* must be given,
Why not a *female* power reside in heaven?
Tho' many vices taint the female breast,
They're not so gross as man's—tho' bad's the best,
'Tis not in virtue, or superior sense;
In Brutal sense consist man's excellence.
Is there a difference of sex in mind?
Those who affirm it must be gravel-blind.
In wit, in genius, and perception true,
There's not a straw to choose between the two.
Yet Eve stands foremost in the first-made couple,
By mustering courage up to eat the apple;†
While *Mister Adam*, like a sneaking cur,
Ate afterward, and laid the blame on her;
But jabbering Paul bids women all obey,
And who to such a jabberer dare say nay?
This saint, says Voltaire, had a mutton fist,
And would have women thumped as well as kissed;
But this in Æsop's fables is explained,
Where Leo to the boasting man complain'd.‡

Or if the YAHOO needs must thump his craw,
Could not the glorious orb attention draw,
Whose splendid beams diffuse both warmth and light,
Without which all would be eternal night?

* What delectable employment for a Deity, to be eternally watching such contemptible grubs in all their silly and wicked actions night and day! And what *heavenly* gratification to behold forty or fifty thousand animals, upon two stumps (to say nothing of the horses; they, poor things, are not blessed with immortal souls), who are cutting one another to atoms in his holy name, and with his embassadors for bottle-holders!

† "Here," says she "you cowardly, faint-hearted wretch, take this heavenly fruit, eat, and be a stupid fool no longer; eat, and become wise; eat, and be a god; and know, to your eternal shame, that your wife has been made an enlightened goddess before you."—*History of the Devil.*

‡ Fable of the Lion and the Man.

Instead of mumbling over such hum-drum,
Unmeaning silly stuff as "kingdom come,"
About the Father-god "*which* art in heaven—"
(English no parish-boy would have forgiven).
But then the Sun a maker had, he'll say:
Suppose it—but who made that maker pray?
Oh, he's *self-existent!* then's the cry;
Obscurium per obscurius, I reply.—
In metaphysic subtleties thus crossed,
The further we jog on the more we're lost.*
Discussed eternally, it still appears,
Like Paddy's ale to thicken as it clears.
But grant man's form divine, on Bible proof;
Is not the composition wretched stuff?
Annoyed by winter's cold and summer's heat,
Which brings by turns kibed heels and sweaty feet,†
How does the learned Smellfungus‡ describe
The imperfections of the YAHOO tribe?
Not riff-raff in St. Giles's cellars bred,
But tip-top quality, by fashion led;
Ladies and lords, in Bath assembly rooms,
Where YAHOO stinks are mingled with perfumes.
"It was indeed," says he, "a compound vile,
Which any parish hog would smell a mile:
Imagine then extremes of stink and sweet,
From Lavender and musk, and dirty feet;
Imposthumated lungs and rotten teeth;
Hartshorn, salvolatile, and stinking breath;
Sour belchings, running sores, and putrid gums:"§

* The king of Prussia, Frederick II., used to say, a metaphysician was like a well-digger—the deeper he went the more he was in the dark.

† "No earthly joys are found complete;
The winter's cold and summer's heat,
Produce kibed heels and sweaty feet."—*Old Ballad.*

‡ Dr. Smollett, so named by Sterne.

§ If the reader should be a little squeamish, and disgusted with Dr. Smellfungus's description of the Yahoo's defects, he is requested to cleanse and purify his imagination by reading Rabshakah's delicate *mag* about eating "their own dung and drinking their own ——" (2 Kings, chap. xviii.); and which, being a choice morsel of holy instruc-

(It's well he does not mention *fiddle-bums!*
Since lords and dukes, with all their fine-dressed doxies,
Must carry with 'em *there* their civet boxes);
"Rank arm-pits, plaisters, assafœtida,
Issues, and bergamot, *et cetera;*
From which effluvia rises to the nose,
But not ambrosial, you may well suppose!
No! frowsy steams, with odors mixed arise,
That might defy old Nick to analyze."*
Such is the portrait of the YAHOO tribe;
Drawn, *après Nature*, by a learned scribe;
One of the M. P. corps, who ought to know
The animal throughout from top to toe.
It may be said, 'twould make a Caffre spew;
Perhaps it might—'tis not for that less true.
Denied it may be, with an awkward grace;
But then the conscience flies up in the face.
Gladly such galling truths would be denied:
CREATION'S LORDS!! to be thus mortified!
So wise! so good! immortal too, and stink so!
Who but a beastly wretch could ever think so!†
But if not true, why are perfumers' shops
Crowded from morn till night with belles and fops?
Who purchase essence with their idle pence,
To smother stinks which give themselves offence.
Except one vile, filthy four-legged creature,§

tion, is again brought upon the tapis in Isaiah, chap. xxvi.; and also to turn to the inspired gibberish called Leviticus and Deuteronomy, where he may read of scabs, issues, running sores, blood, guts, and unclean things, chapter after chapter, to his great delight and edification,, without its producing any tendency to squeamishness or *boaking;* this being all the word of God, is gulped down like barley-sugar, even by novel-reading ladies, on the Lord's day! So that it is not the "what is it?" but the "who says it?" that determines the matter; as it is not to be supposed possible for a Holy Ghost to talk filthily.

* The whole assemblage, it should seem by the learned doctor's account, might with great propriety have exclaimed with the lunatic prophet, "we are all as an *unclean thing.*"—Isaiah, lxiv., 6.

† See "Clarke's Critical Review."

‡ "Painted for sight, and essenced for the smell,
Sail in the ladies."—*Donne.*

§ The Skunk, or Stinkbissem, an animal hunted sometimes at the

There's nothing so offensive in its nature.
A pretty demi-god to swell and strut!
Corruption as he is from head to foot!
A bundle of infirmities at best,
Altho' in velvet robes and ermine dressed,
And stars and baubles glitter at his breast!
But then he has a SOUL, a spark divine!
That oozes thro' the filthy mass to shine!
Tant pis, alas! since nine are out of ten
Picked up by BLACKEY for his blazing den;
Where, being *immaterial*, they fume
And frizzle, day and night, but ne'er consume!
Now, why should this scrub want so many souls
Which in war time must people hell in shoals?*
Can he have sugar-canes to cultivate?
Or sulphur-mines to work on his estate?
Or is it malice to his adversary,
That spurs him on poor YAHOO's soul to worry?
Without some motive would he take such pains
And sweat and fag, and rack his sooty brains?
And like a roaring lion, trot about
Continually to smell poor YAHOOS out?
No; like the biped, he'd not stir for nought,
Nor give a penny but to gain a groat.†

cape of Good Hope, which, when hard pressed by the dogs, lets fly from its rump-battery such a pestiferous volley of stink-pots, or rather stink-shots, that the dogs are obliged to turn tail, overcome by the suffocating stench.

"De toutes nos secretions," says Voltaire, "il n'y en a pas une seule qui soit bonne à rein; pas une seule même qui ne rende le genre humain disagréable."—*Questions*. Voltaire is, however, mistaken in his assertion: urine is valuable to dyers, chemists, printers, and others; and the fœces is now found to be of great utility, and even advertised for as an article for exportation, under the delicate denomination of *Dessicated Compost*, at so much per hogshead, and particularly recommended to the West India merchants for the improvement of their sugar-cane.—See *The Times*, of April, 1826, and since.

* ——"The greatest chief
That ever peopled hell with heroes slain."—*Byron*.

† ——"We found no bait
To tempt us in thy country. Doing good,
Disinterested good, is not our trade;
We travel far, 'tis true, but not for naught."—*Cowper*.

The YAHOO, ignorant of Nature's laws,
Presumes himself to be a final cause:
"Sun, moon, and stars," he cries, "and earth and sea,
Are all created but to pleasure me."
But is not Gay's fleas' logic just as good,
Who deems the man made only for *his* food?*
The parson says, indeed, he's but a worm;
But still he's modelled on Jehovah's form.
Jehovah's form, poor wretch, 'tis very plain,
Excess of pride has addled his poor brain.
When of his *godlike* qualities he raved,
His heated noddle should be closely shaved:
Endowed with cunning, tho' devoid of sense,
He hides what gives his vanity offence,†
Or tries tries to hide it, rather, should be said,
Like the poor ostrich, who conceals his head;
And when this vice he can no longer hide,
'Tis brazened out, and then called *decent* pride.
But what is decent? what does decent mean?
Just what we please; 'tis nothing but a screen—
A trick, a subterfuge, a sophist's cavil,
To make vice virtue, and to cheat the Devil.
Yes, shuffle and disguise it how we will,
'Tis pride and envy rule the Yahoo still;
Abstracted from these passions, we shall find
'Tis but a lifeless lump that's left behind:‡

* Gay's Fables.—See Voltaire's excellent *Discours sur l'Homme.*

† "L'orgueil est égal dans tous les hommes, et il n'y a point de difference qu'aux moyens, et à la manière de le mettre au jour."—*Rochefoucault.*

‡ If it were possible to take pride and envy from the human species, grass would soon grow in Bond street and Cheapside. "Man without envy and pride," says Mandeville, "may, with great propriety, be compared to a log in a pond, with but little inclination to exert himself."—*Fable of the Bees.* Horace Walpole remarks, that "envy, though one of the worst and meanest of our passions, seems *somehow* natural to the human breast."—*Walpoliana.* Smollett says, "I am inclined to think no mind was ever wholly exempt from envy, which, perhaps, may have been implanted as an instinct essential to our nature." And Arbuthnot, speaking of party violence, upon the death of *Brandy Nan*, says, in a letter to Swift, "I have an opportunity, calmly and philosophically, to consider that treasure of vileness and baseness that

Take pride and envy from the belles and fops,
The bauble-venders soon must shut their shops.
Like other animals decreed by fate
To eat, and drink, and sleep, and propagate.
But for his *rationality*, his boast,
If ever he possessed it, 'tis now lost.
REASON! oh, name it not; 'tis profanation:*
The *reasonable* YAHOO fears damnation;
The *reasonable* Christian is baptized;
The *reasonable* Jew is circumcised:
(For by the *holy* snipcock operation,†
The Lord will recognise the "chosen nation"‡
When the last trumpet sounds, and all like bears,
Are scrambling for their bones to get up stairs:)§
The Christian infant's made a babe of grace,
By having water sprinkled on his face;
(Quære, would not the holy water tell,
If sprinkled on the backside, just as well?
The OLD ONE might be skulking thereabout,

I always believed to be in the heart of man."—"Notre envie," observes Rochefoucault, "dure toujours plus long temps que le bonheur de ceux que nous envions."

* "Ce qui est le plus contraire a la droite *Raison* c'est cela même apres quoi on court le plus avidement. Demandez vous pourquoi? C'est que presque tous les hommes sont Fous."—*Erasme.*

† "Le prepuce est coupé en cérémonie à l'age de huit ans [the holy book says eight days] on a porté dans quelques-unes de nos villes le *saint* prépuce en procession; on le garde encore dans quelques sacristies, sans que cette facetie ait causé le moindre trouble dans les familles."—*Questions.*

‡ "For thou art a holy people unto the Lord thy God: the Lord hath chosen thee to be a special people unto himself, above all people that are upon the face of the earth."—Deut. vii. They might have been "the chosen people," said Lord Rochester:—

"But why the devil they were chose,
The Lord himself sure only knows;"

as from their beastly conduct, it might have been supposed they were the devil's leavings.

§ As we see God "in the flesh" (Job xix.) the bones must be wanted of course. This is, however, contrary to the assertion of St. Paul, who says, "flesh and blood can not inherit the kingdom of God."—1 Cor. xv.

And then the cross would keep the rascal out;)
While some more learned, solemn, owl-phizzed fools,
Well crammed with rubbish from the lumber-schools,*
Baptize the *unborn* infant with a squirt,
Without the child or mother being hurt!†
What *reasonable* conduct! are all right,
Jews, Turks, and Christians too, are all delight
For this whene'er they meet, to scratch and fight.‡
What reverend harpies! what a brawling crew!
In all their deeds the cloven-foot peeps through;
Fraught with the musty tenants of a college,
These self-dubbed *wranglers* boast their classic knowledge,
No wonder they the heathens do despise,
Since *they* to Christian doctrines shut their eyes;
No *blessed* Gospel in their skulls was crammed,
For want of which (thank God) they're now all damned:
Had they been blessed, like us, with Gospel-light in
Their noddles, they'd (saint-like) have gone to smiting.

Oh, *blessed Gospel*-like! who'd e'er suppose
From such *pure* light that saints should come to blows?
Yet such are Evangelicals; who boast
Of being crop-crammed with the Holy Ghost!
The jargon of the frothy spouter Paul,
Bothers the pericraniums of them all.
"Cast off the old man," Mawworm cries; "'tis plain,
You must be damned unless you're *born again*."
Some howl for grace, some for predestination,
Some for election, some for reprobation.§
Aloud you'll hear a praise-God Barebones bawl,

* "Filling frantic crowds of learned fools
Those reverend bedlams, colleges, and schools."—*Lord Rochester.*

† "The doctors of the Sorbonne have decreed, that though no part of the child's body should appear, it may be baptized by injection: par le moyen d'une petite canulle, sans faire tort a la mére."—*T. Shandy.*

‡ "Par piété ils se traitent mutuellent de blasphemateurs et d'impies."—*Volney.*

§ The reader who may wish for amusement as well as information from the holy gibberish, is referred to Clarke's excellent *Critical Review.*

"Ye're muttons lost, unless ye have a call!
And so are they who of their good works brag,
Self-righteousness is but a filthy rag.
Sweet Jesus only sinners must confide in,
And guard against 'short-comings,' and 'backsliding.'
Without faith in the *Lamb* to hell you'll go;
But Lamb's blood washes you as *white* as snow."

All full of Jesus, each light-headed sect
Boasts loudly of their "spread of intellect."
From gospel-light, or rather gospel-dung,*
What crops of muddled nincompoops have sprung!
Hernhutters, Jumpers, Ranters, Harmonites,
Revivers, Squatters, Calvinists, New Lights,
Arminians, Quakers, Muggletonians,
Socinians, Anabaptists, Antinomians,
Swedenborgs, Arians, Shil-Southcotites;
The major part rank fools, the rest rank bites.

Such are the Christian YAHOOS, who delight
To blindfold reason with their *inward* light.†
Peter and Paul are conned; but, still perplexed,
They rummage Luke, and Mark, and Matthew next:
From text to text the pious buzzards fly,
While "the land stinks, so num'rous are the fry."
Yet some of these pure saints *now* seem to think

* Whitefield, in one of his ranting sermons, at Glasgow, in the year 1742, thus expresses himself: "O Lord, dung us with Jesus Christ, that we bring forth much fruit for thee." — See *Lewis's Memoirs.* And in writing to Lady Huntingdon, the same preacher of the blessed gospel says, "I have just now risen from the ground, after praying to the Lord of all lords to water your soul every moment, honored madam."—*Southey's Wesley.* Tom Brown quotes the following prayer from one of the frothy spouters in his time: "Souse us, O Lord, in the powdering-tub of thy grace, that we may become tripes fit for thy heavenly table; sweeten us with the sugar-candy of thy mercy, O Lord, that we may all be rendered lollypops and bull's-eyes for the righteous in kingdom come!"

† "'Tis such a light as putrefaction breeds
In fly-blown flesh, whereon the maggot feeds;
Shines in the dark, but ushered into day,
The stench remains the lustre dies away."
Cowper.

Young girls may too much in the bible squint:
And stumbling upon passages obscene,*
Must wonder what such paw-paw words can mean.

Does holy church then hatch such precious crops?
Or are they cuddled in old blackey's shops?
Whence can such crowds of frantic fools proceed?
From gospel! yes, they're all of gospel breed.
While pious tracts of "Christ and Crusts" abound.†
Saints are in every hole and corner found
We're so be-sanctified, so truly blest,
So gospel-gorged, poor Mawworm can not rest;
But starts red-hot, a missionary bite,
Eager to give poor heathens *gospel-light:*
Poor Mawworm finds more pigs than teats at home,
So ventures forth 'mongst infidels to roam,
To preach to Ashantees God's holy word,
To kick out Scratch, and introduce the Lord;
Tho' by his pious efforts it appears
He sets them altogether by the ears:
For tho' the man of God no labor spares,
Nick will amongst the wheat still sow his tares.

Ye pious missionaries! let us know
How many are converted where you go;
And whether, while ye in your lingo prate,
The Holy Ghost stands by ye to translate.
In your next kind communications tell us,
Whether the Lord of savages is jealous.‡

* Teaching the poor to read so generally has cut out plenty of employment for the spiritual sow-gelders, who are now as busy as the devil in a high wind in grubbing out the impurities from the holy balderdash, lest their chaste female devotees might now and then be shocked by reading so often about "going in unto her," &c.

† The title of a favorite tract, originating in the answer of a poor woman, who, when asked by an evangelical lady, if she was in want of anything replied, "No, my dear madam, thank the Lord; I never can be in want of anything while I have my Christ and my crust."

‡ "Thou shalt have no other gods but me: for I, the Lord, am a *jealous* God," &c. If the great Jehovah was jealous in regard to the worship of such a tribe of filthy, stinking, hungruffin snipcocks, as his favorites appear to have been, it is not to be wondered if he were also and *likewise* respecting the prayers and supplications of the Catabaws, Ottogamies, &c., when addressed to the Great Spirit in the cavern.

And whether, when ye treat them with rum-grog,
They're not for holy gospel more agog;
And oft come after baptism rather mellow,
Roaring out, " Goramity, damned good fellow!
More grog, good massa pardon, more baptize:"*
Then aren't ye struck with horror and surprise
To hear them, when they're told the *Lamb* is God,
And that their sins are washed out by his blood,
Cry out, " Oh, Benamuckee! massa parson, fie!
Dat wat you preach be one big God-dam lie;
For if young litel Goramity *Lamb*,
Den great old Goramity be de *Ram*."

Oh, reverend leeches! ere the world ye roam,
Why not convert the infidels at home?
Is all your credit with Jehovah lost?
Have you no Shiloh, nor a Cock-lane ghost?
Why not *let off* a miracle or two?
A subject from the churchyard raised would do;
Or send a man to walk, as it is said
Saint Denis did in France, without his head;
Something to terrify and make us stare,
And tumble on our marrow-bones to prayer;
Something to put the rabble in a quaking:
The Lord, no doubt, would bless the undertaking;
Since ye all fag and labor for his church,
He can't in conscience leave you in the lurch.
Try what your praying to the *Lamb* can do,
And bring a ghost or bugaboo to view:
As ye're all blessed with faith, ye can not doubt
But what the Lord at last will help ye out;
Nor turn his back upon such holy men,
Who feast upon his carcass now and then.

Witch-hunting Jamie, a true Lord's anointed,

* Horace Walpole (speaking of China) says, "This China is indeed a bad dose: hundreds of millions are there seen who have never heard of Christ of Judea.

"Even the *Salvator Mundi* died to no purpose! only to save the hundredth part of a fraction! What an insult to the faith! We ought to have a crusade against those Chinese, and baptize them in their blood, by all means—the shocking infidels!"—*Walpoliana.*

As ever by the Devil was appointed,*
Was by the Gospel-preaching vampires told
The "word of God" was better than pure gold;
That lucre, and the riches of the earth,
Were dross, compared with such transcendent worth.†
(They should have said, this "pearl above all price"
Enabled saints to live in sloth and vice.)‡
But tho' it proves such to these reverend leeehes,
Who chouse the rabble with their pulpit-speeches;
And who, by virtue of the "holy word,"
Cram their fat paunches, and cry, "Fear the Lord;"
Is it not to the laity a curse?
Could Belzebub have ever sent a worse?
Has it not set, wherever it was known,
Wife against husband, father against son?
To love your wife or child's a grand mistake—
You're taught to hate each other for Christ's sake.§
Take no thought for to-day; and when you die,
The dead may bury you, or there you lie.‖
"Compel them to come in," the parsons bawl,
Or excommunicate them one and all.
Wo be to those whom they dare trample on,
For where they have the power they spare none.
Lift but a finger at the sacred sty,
"The church—the church's in danger!" they all cry
Wherever *filthy lucre* much abounds,

* "If such kings were by God appointed,
The Devil might be the Lord's anointed."—*Lord Rochester.*

† See the canting, fawning, fulsome, toad-eating, lick-spittle, and true priestly dedication of the translators of the *blessed book* to the British Solomon.

‡ "Qui legit historiam ecclesiasticam, quid legit," says Grotius, "nisi vitia episcoporum?"

§ "I am come to send fire on the earth." (Very like a benevolent Deity!) "Suppose ye that I come to give peace? I tell ye nay; but rather division: the father shall be divided against the son, and the son against the father; the mother against the daughter, and the daughter against the mother."—Luke xii.

‖ "And he said unto another, Follow me. But he said, Lord, suffer me first to go and bury my father. Jesus said unto him, Let the dead bury the dead, but go thou and preach."—Luke ix.

The pack are on the scent like staunch fox-hounds;
Wealth to obtain, their Machiavelian plan
Is to promote dissension where they can.
Do different sects in friendship e'er unite?
No; Christ's disciples all like tigers fight.
The LAMBKIN said he came to bring a sword,*
And, *Lamb* like Christians use it for their Lord.

Oh! had the YAHOO eyes, he'd plainly see
What bitter fruit grows on the Gospel tree;
What pestilential crabs have ever grown,
And ever will, where'er this tree is known.
Look round the Globe—for near two thousand years,
The CROSS has deluged it with blood and tears;†
Nor will the YAHOO happier days e'er find,
While he with Gospel-light continues blind:
His intellect may *march*, as he supposes,
But in the mud 'twill stick with Christ and Moses.
Of real intellect there'll be no spread,
Till such stuff's driven from his bother'd head.

With few-faw-fum and mummery beguiled,
The YAHOO's brains are addled when a child;
And when adult, he learns from godly books,
The Lord's best pleased when he has dismal looks.
The Christian's *blessed* has *cursed* the earth,‡
And brought them strife and war, instead of mirth.
The *tidings* far from making them all glad,§
Gives them the doldrums, and drives thousands mad.
Doesn't Augustine (the greatest saint who brought

* "Think not that I am come to bring peace on earth; I am come not to send peace, but a sword."—Matt. x.

† "The scene of Christianity has always been a scene of dissension, of hatred, of persecution, and of blood.—*Bolingbroke.* And what says Erasmus: "Sanguin fundata est ecclesia, sanguin crevit, sanguin succrevit, sanguin erit."

‡ "Among other precious relics," says Mr. Walpole, "which we were treated with the sight of at this convent, we were shown a piece of the *blessed* fig-tree which our guide said had been cursed by Christ." —*Walpole's Correspondence.*

§ "O thou that bringest good tidings to Zion!"

The precious twaddle here which we're all taught,)
With Jerome, Cyprian, and Tertullian too,
Pronounce us damn'd if pleasure we pursue ?*
Did not the pious Origen, to save him
From Nick's claws, cut off what Jehovah gave him ?
And thus escaping from the OLD ONE's gripe,
Sing hallelujahs with soprano pipe !
For had he been by woman led astray,
He must to *kingdom-come* have lost his way ;
Since Jerome tells us ! that *their* very touch
Is worse than mad dog's bite, their venom's such !†
Doesn't the LAMB himself, such joys despising,
Hold forth in favor of this *eunuchizing ?*‡
Hence parsons, tho' so given to caterwauling,
'Gainst "sinful lust o' the flesh" are always bawling.
A cheerful look denotes a want of grace ;
John Bunyan wears no smile upon his face ;
John bids us groan and pray, and sob and howl ;
For should you not, Nick nabs your sinful soul.

Unhappy Cowper ! tho' with genius blest,
By this true Christian nightmare was opprest :
His mind infected with the curse, he cries,
"The cross, the cross alone can make us wise !"§
Has not this cross, this emblem of salvation,
Rendered this life a temporal damnation
Is not a crucifix a horrid sight ?
Yet Christian YAHOOS view it with delight !
A naked man upon a gibbet nail'd,

* See "Gibbon's Decline and Fall," chap. xv.

† See note on dancing, in the conclusion.

‡ "And there be eunuchs which have made themselves eunuchs for the kingdom of heaven's sake."—Matt. xix.

§ Yes, if lunacy is wisdom. This horrid emblem of Christianity has transformed the poor *Yahoos* into blood-drinking tigers. Will it be credited, that representations of the detestable crucifixion used to take place on Good Friday in some of the convents in Paris, when infatuated women (perhaps prepared by opium) ,were actually nailed by their hands and feet to a *cross!* in which horrid state they were kept several hours? One poor creature expired in agony, after drawing out the nails from her hands and feet.—*See Baron Grimm's Correspondence.*

4

By squeamish girls is e'en with rapture hail'd!
They call it *Lamb, Sweet Jesus, and Dear Savior!*
And out-rant Bedlamites by their behavior.

See surly Johnson frightened by a dream,
Come roaring like the monster Polypheme;
He heard his mother in the night call "*Sam*,"*
And heard himself say, "Mother, here I am!"
A back-bone Christian, gloomy and uncivil—
Praying to God, and trembling at the Devil.
With superstition haunted day and night,
He dreamt of ghosts, and hags, and second-sight:
Credits old silly women's tales of witches,
Who once to Bozzy he affirm'd were bitches.†
His long-tail'd words astound the gaping mob,
Who think the Doctor had a wond'rous nob.
Bow-wowing triads, like a mastiff-dog,‡
And in politeness distanced by a hog;
Irascible and savage in debate,
Thwart him, perhaps you risk'd a broken pate
Rouse Ursus-Major, and in growling tones,
He threatens *a la Crib* to break your bones.§
Yet tho' to manners he has no pretence,
He is call'd *the* MORALIST, *par excellence!*
The Doctor knew the *gang*, 'tis very plain,
And he puff'd those who puff'd up him again.‖

* See "Boswell's Life of Johnson."

† "Naught proved the non-existence of the bitches."—*Bozzy and Pozzy.*

‡ "Lord Pembroke said once to me at Wilton, with happy pleasantry and some truth, that Dr. Johnson's sayings would not appear so extraordinary were it not for his *bow wow* way."—*Boswell's Life of Johnson.*

§ The Doctor was told Foote had an intention of caricaturing his hoggish manners and pompous fustian on the stage. "If the dog does," (the usual expression of the great Christian moralist,) says he, "I'll break every bone in his skin."—See *Lexiphanes.* Surly Sam, alias Rhinoceros, had knocked down ———, a bookseller in the Row, who had offended him, and of which he frequently boasted.

‖ The Doctor, however, was not always "up to snuff" in this particular, and till his apostacy neither obtained pudding nor praise. In the first edition of his lumbering Dictionary, the word Pension was

He's now a demi-saint; but few shine brighter,
Either as a Gospel-sniveller, or smiter.
YAHOO, admire thy hoggish Christian brother;
'Tis natural for hogs to like each other.

Does not the gloomy "Night Thoughts" Young declare,
That Christians all should spend their time in prayer?
That laughter's half immoral, and that song,*
And dance, and mirth, to Beelzebub belong?

defined, "the pay of a state-hireling for treason against his country." See *Lexiphanes*, page 24, note. But as this was not the way to procure a sop in the pan, the great moralist wheeled to the right about, roared to a contrary tune, and naturally superstitious, bespattered the church party with adulation, perceiving the great influence they possessed in society, and their power to puff up or suppress any one by their reviews or other publications, as they might think fit. With this party he soon succeeded; and as all his writings were in favor of church and state, he was not overlooked by those in power, and soon obtained a pension of £300 per annum, and became in a short time the "*great Dr. Johnson.*" And as Dr. Shebbeare was pensioned at the same period, it gave rise to a sarcastic joke, that the king kept two bears, a he-bear and a she-bear. The following descriptive lines of the *great moralist*, by Churchill, may not be unacceptable to the reader:—

"POMPOSO, insolent and loud,
Vain idol of a *scribbling* crowd:
Whose very name inspires an awe;
Whose every word is sense and law;
Who, cursing flattery, is the tool
Of every fawning, flattering fool;
Who proudly seized of *Learning's* throne,
Now damns all learning but his own;
And makes each sentence current pass,
With *puppy, coxcomb, scoundrel, ass.*
For 'tis with him a certain rule,
The folly's proved when he calls fool:
Who, to increase his native strength,
Draws words six syllables in length,
With which, assisted by his frown,
By way of club, he knocks us down!
His comrades' terrors to beguile,
Grins horribly a ghastly smile:
Features so horrid, were it light,
Would put the Devil himself to flight."

See *The Ghost.*

* "Laughter itself is half immoral;
Pardon a thought that seems severe."—*Night Thoughts.*

That sublunary pleasures tend to evil,*
And lead backsliding sinners to the Devil?
Hence Holy-Bible grubbers quail and quake,
Scared at the "wrath to come," and "fiery lake;"
Hence saints have all such sad Good-Friday faces
Peepers turn'd up, long jaws, and queer grimaces:
If singing psalms with godly spunk o'erflowing,
They sing as if they to the DROP were going.
(Whether the Lord loves music there's no saying,
But sure he can not love such asses' braying!
Such lullabies, tho' meant to compliment him,
And to his "praise and glory" must torment him;
When their vile snuffling, dismal strains he hears
No doubt in haste he buttons up his ears.)†
All day by old Scratch haunted, in a fright
They go to bed, and dream of hell at night.
The "sinfulness of sin" so much prevails,‡
They think the Devil's always at their tails.§

* "When pleasure's seized, compute your mighty gains;
What is it but rank poison in your veins?"—*Young's Satires.*

☞ So sings this sanctified, wo-stricken son of the church, who, under the heaviest denunciations against worldly pleasures, and the sin of participating in them, hunted after "*filthy lucre,*" and the "mammon of unrighteousness," with the greediness of a dragon. See a curious letter of the Rev. Doctor's, in the whining way to Lady Suffolk, (when Mrs. Howard,) in *The Mirror*, No. 78: and also his toad-eating blarney to Silly Bub,* Sir Roberty Walpole, the Duke of Dorset, &c., &c., in his Satires and Dedications.

† "And yet how many a voice, and pipe, and chord,
Bray to the praise and glory of the Lord!
How merciful is Heaven to bear such pother,
And not knock one thick skull against the other!"
P. Pindar.

‡ A favorite expression of the Mawworn tribe.

§ "A look of horror spread all o'er 'em,
As if they saw hell-fire before 'em;
And Satan with a sable pack
Of long-tail'd devils at his back,
Ready with pitchforks to begin
To push 'em all by dozens in."—*Homer Burlesqued.*

* Bubb Doddington, it is said, complained of his Christian name to Lord Chesterfield, who advised him to prefix Silly to it.

Such saints may smile perhaps in "kingdom come,"
But here on earth they look confounded glum;
And tho' they fear not Satan, they all cry,
Their dismal phizzes give their tongues the lie.
You'd think such *Lamb*-like saints could never fight;
But when the heathens meet, they're bound to smite.
Cutting their throats who don't believe the *Word*,
Is "laboring in the vineyard of the Lord;"
And smiting infidels, and Jews, and Turks,
Rank foremost in a Christian's holy works.
  Does conscience check him? No; he boasts the deed:
Infants, if heretics, are doom'd to bleed.
(Jehovah's butchers are not over nice;
"Nits," they exclaim, "in time will grow to lice.")*
The saint exults—his parson eggs him on,
And tells him all he kill'd to hell are gone.
What's conscience, then? A fudge of putty made;
To murder for the *Lamb* no saint's afraid.
Conscience is taught to slumber at such times;
There's no remorse felt for religious crimes.†
The saints beg God will give them strength and grace,
For smiting "hip and thigh" the heathen race;
And should th' ungodly ever come in view,
That "over Edom they might cast their shoe,"‡
"O blessed Lord!" the Gospel blood-hounds cry,
(Their verjuiced *mugs* all turn'd tow'rds the sky,)
"To smite the infidels, oh! grant that we
In thine hands humble instruments may be!
Permit us in thy name to cut off all
Of Ahab's race that p—s against the wall;§
Like holy Samuel in thy name to smite,‖

* A common expression when children were murdered at Paris, on St. Bartholomew's eve, as well as in the Irish massacre.—See *Mr. Macauley's History of England*, year 1641.

† "Tantum religio potuit suadere malorum."—*Lucretius.*

‡ "Over Edom will I cast out my shoe."—Psalm lx.

The custom of throwing the shoe, or striking a person with it, seems to be continued in the East till the present day.—See *Hadji Baba.*

§ 2 Kings ix.

‖ "And Samuel hewed Agag in pieces before the Lord."—1 Sam. xv. 33.

And to our knees in blood for thee to fight.
A Bible in their hands, the godly crew
Have a "carte-blanche" for whatsoe'er they do:
All full of "praise-God-zeal," they smite away,
Then drop upon their marrow-bones to pray.
Oh, Fate, pray keep all Mawworm Christians from me,
For where they come they play up Hell and Tommy!*
Thou *non com.* biped! boast your holy trash—
Your Bible-calipee and calipash;
Your Blessed Trinity, where One is Three,
And orthodox and lunatic agree!
Mix'd up with humbug, fudge, and contradiction,

* A proverbial expression, signifying skylarking, rowing, going it, or kicking up a rumpus, or a bobbery; and particularly applicable to assemblages of squabbling, crack-brained fanatics, which always end in riots and confusion; *e. g.* (among many others) a meeting was held at the London Tavern, a short time since, for religious discussion between the Catholics (who, it appeared, had been challenged by their adversaries) and the Methodists, or Evangelicals, two squads holy, *par excellence*, when Miss Tisiphone and her godly bickerings, and hell and Tommy was played up in style. Swift, speaking of the wrangling fiddlers, says,

"Strange that such difference should be,
'Twixt tweedle-dum and tweedle-dee."

May we not say also,

'Tis strange such *hellish* wrath should rise
'Twixt *heavenly* saints of kingdom come;
While one gang *hocus pocus* cries,
The other bawls for *fee faw fum.*

When in the heat of the debate, fisty-cuffs commenced; and, in the words of the so much admired Greek poet,

"Some clench'd their fists, and then would dart 'em,
At others' nobs, *secundem artem;*
While some got punches in their stomachs,
Others got kicks which gave 'em bumachs."

The "argumentum baculinum" was then resorted to, and a generous *hubbubboo* ensued. The Methodist party, by far the most numerous, vociferating, "Down with 'em? Break the necks of the ungodly! Show 'em a short way from Dan to Beersheba!" Meaning, that the *Papishes*, as they were called, should be thrown over the staircase; which, in their red hot fits of godly zeal, would have taken place, but for the interference of the constables, who had been called in to prevent further mischief; the chairman of the Evangelicals, Mr. P., roaring out like a bull all the time to "*comprehend* all *as* made a disturbance," although it was entirely occasioned by their own party.

Surpassing all th' extravagance of fiction :
Incomprehensibles amalgamate
With all the rubbish in your chok'd up pate ;
Whatever is impossible believe—
'Tis holy logic, and can ne'er deceive.*
Saint Athanasius, pitying your condition,
This nostrum found to save you from perdition,
Which must prove efficacious, understood,
Especially to noddles full of mud :—
Three Gods are seen by all possessed of grace,
As plainly as the nose upon your face ;
The conjuror comes, with " Presto, fly, begone !"
And lo, they're metamorphosed into *one !*
But in the hodge-podge, mixty-maxty mess,
Which are th' efficient, we are left to guess ;
And therefore, when we pray, we ought to know
If it should not be to the Lord and Co.

But why on three Gods only do you fix,
Since you so oft acknowledge five or six ?
Why elbow out, against all common sense,
So rudely, Nature, Heav'n, and Providence ?
There's not a day but what, with turn'd-up eyes,
You these as deities apostrophize.
And then so ungallant, so like a bear,
To oust thus (fie upon you) *Madame Mere !*
Across the Channel there's your YAHOO brother,
Admits the Virgin in the firm as Mother ;†
While you with gloomy Calvinistic snout,
In college fashion, turn the lady out ;‡

* "Credo," says the lunatic, Tertullian, "quia impossibile est."—"Il n'est rien cru si fermement que ce qu'on sçait le moins, ni gens si asseurez que ceux qui nous content des fables."—*Montaigne.*

† "If the Virgin Mary is not comprised in the Trinity, she is at least worshipped and more idolized than the third Person, alias the Ghost."—See *Smollett's Travels.*

‡ Several places are held in the universities by bachelors only, who forfeit them by marrying ; and the same popish custom is observed at Lambeth, where archbishops' *train bearers* (what true Christian humility !) are dismissed if they marry.

And leave with all your holy orthodoxy,
The blessed Trinity without a doxy.

Æsop's poor heathen had a god and beat him;*
Enlighten'd Christians make a God and eat him:
Christ's flesh and blood is by the faithful taken,†
And gulph'd down just like so much beer and bacon.
But when this holy stuff is in the crop,
Does it for ever undigested stop?
Or does the sacramental *peck* and *booze*,
Thro' chitterlings with other matter ooze?
By peristaltic motion groping on,
All its soul-purifying virtues gone?
And then, in this contaminated state,
Be turn'd out rudely at the postern gate?‡
Sure, spawn'd from hell's dark pit, some wretched dreamer,
First thought of gobbling up his "dear Redeemer?"

Oh! heaven-born YAHOO! sure thy Christianity
Is folly's "ne plus ultra," or insanity!
Who but an idiot, or a bedlamite,
Could take such diet, and with such delight?
Then, like a *faithful* sacrament receiver,
Thunder damnation on each unbeliever.
Egregious dolt! would any but a stark ass,
First make a God, then pray upon his carcass?
The "paragon of animals," indeed!§

* Fable of the man and his Wooden God.

† "The body and blood of Christ, [a dainty dish for a Yahoo!] which is *verily* and indeed taken and received by the *faithful* in the Lord's Supper." Among other lunatic sects of Christians who delighted in gobbling up their Maker, there was one who used to mix the blood of children in their sacramental wine! Another "body and blood" crew had a custom of cramming ailing infants with a sacramental bread, at the risk of choking them, with a view of saving them from the Devil!—See *Bailey*, word "Cataphyrgians," and "Moral Philosopher," vol. i., p. 113.

‡ "Mais mon cher ami," lui dit l'Empereur, "tu as mangé et bu ton Dieu, que deviendra t'il quand tu auras besoin d'un pot de chambre?"—"Sire," dit frere Rigolet, "il deviendra ce qu'il pourra: c'est son affaire."—*Dialogue entre l'Empereur de la Chine et Jesuite.*

§ Shakspere.

On the Lord's "flesh and blood" like hogs to feed!
Then wipe their muzzles, and come raving forth,
To murder heathens in their Christian wrath:
Nor is it infidels alone they smite,
The pious Christians one another bite;*
Each sect upbraids the rest with superstition,†
And boast their wisdom in this cursed condition!
Thro' all the scale of animated nature,
There is not such another stupid creature!‡
Writs now seem wanted wheresoe'er we go,
Of "inquirendo de lunatico."

Yes; superstition is the Yahoo's curse,
That strips the flock to cram the parson's purse.
When call'd *religion*, it cajoles the weak,§
Who then, from fear of hell, the parson seek;
To Mumbo-jumbo, or grim Juggernaut,
Or Bennamuckee, just as they are taught—
To Moses, or Mohammed, or to Christ;
By superstition one and all enticed:
Each bigot cries, his head with rubbish cramm'd,
"Mine's *true* religion—all the rest are damn'd;"
While church, and synagogue, and mosque, all yell,
And send each other's devotees to hell:

* "For now the war is not between
The brethren and the men of sin;
But saint and saint to spill the blood
Of one another's brotherhood."—*Hudibras.*

"Dans tous les tems on voit les membres de l'Eglise de Dieu disposés à s'arracher les yeux."—*Le Citateur.*

† "Ignorance and fear produced superstition, and superstition in its turn maintained ignorance and fear in the minds of men. Thus, superstition broached the notion of inspiration; and when the notion was once established, and the fact bèlieved, supposed inspiration served to confirm and authorize superstition."—*Bolingbroke's Philosophical Essays.*

‡ "J'ai augmenté l'ouvrage d'un volume, que les sottises humaines m'ont fourni: c'est une source inepuisable."—*Le Sage.* And Gibbon, in his posthumous works, observes, that "man is the greatest fool of the whole creation."

§ Hobbes says, and with great truth, "Religion is a superstition *in* fashion; and superstition is a religion *out* of fashion."

Encouraged by their priests they smite away,
And murder's soon the order of the day.*
Wherever Superstition's imps have been,
A Golgotha, or place of skulls is seen;
Wherever she has reared her hydra head,
There human blood in torrents has been shed;
Chains, gibbets, racks, and wheels, her steps attend,
And hell-born "Acts of Faith" her throne defend.†
Crusades and Paris massacres proclaim
With Ireland's murders, her infernal fame.

Such are Jehovah's pious, blessed race,
Born "babes of wrath," but changed to "babes of grace:"
Yes, "babes of grace;" and pretty babes they are!
And well they fatten upon Gospel fare.
From *sin original*, the parson's sprinkling
Cleanses the infant Yahoo in a twinkling;
The holy water washes off the sin,
Infuses grace, and makes the devil grin.

Ah! Blackey! you may howl, and grin, and chatter,
(God bless the parson and his holy water;)
Tho' you chous'd Eve and Adam long ago,
We do not care a button for you now.
Yet sure 'tis strange, a rascal like old Scratch,
Should for the great Jehovah be a match!‡
For now HIS ROYAL HIGHNESS well may boast,§

* "Excités par la voix des prêtres sanguinaires,
Invoquaient le seigneur en égorgeant leurs frères."—*Voltaire.*
See *L'Esprit*, Discours 2, chap. 24; also *La Noi Naturelle*, 3me partie.

† Auto-da-fe.—See *Questions*, tom. ii. p. 324.

‡ "Le bon Dieu c'est réellement trompé dans votre système, car s'il avait prevu que son ennemi empoisonnerait ici bas toutes ses œuvres il ne les aurait pas produites; il ne se serait pas préparé lui-meme la honte d'etre continuellement joué et vaincu."—*Questions.*

§ Whether this cock of the walk, who goes about "like a roaring lion," (not the way by-the-bye to lure gulls, one should suppose,) and is acknowledged as Prince of Darkness, is entitled to the appellation of *royal* or *serene* highness, the Herald's College might perhaps determine; and also whether the whole corps of ***** and serenes are not his descendants. But surely he ought not to be deprived of his just and proper titles, nor refused the homage and respect of the Yahoo

That by his cunning Paradise was lost;
Since Eve and Adam both from thence were driven,
Because he got his . . . . kicked out of heaven.

Oh, Johnny Noakes, Tom Tram, and Jack o'Nory,
Assist us to relate this pretty story;
Whicn proves the YAHOO has a precious noddle,
And that he, precious stuff, can in it coddle.

It seems, then, Blackey, full of hellish spite
As well in such a case, indeed he might,
Said to himself, " As sure as my name's Nick,*
I'll play Jehovah some damn'd scurvy trick.
A pretty rig, by God! I'm kicked down stairs,
Because I didn't choose to say my pray'rs,
Or sit contented with my naked rump
Upon a cloud to blow a penny trump:
A chin-cough in that way I've often got,
Sitting without my breeches, like a sot,
Tantara-raring it with all my might,
While cherubims squall'd† " Holy!" day and night;‡
Expecting to be paid, instead of which,
I'm bundled out with kicks upon my breech;

race of whom we are assured he *snaffles* up a decent crop; and who, therefore, ought to be always cap in hand to deprecate his wrath, and ingratiate themselves in his favor, with a view of good usage and a snug birth in his chimney-corner; for, although he is now in the suds, who can say but that he may get his chin above water again some day (as Huet observed, when he bowed to the statue of Jupiter at Rome), and then he might recollect and reward those who had paid their respects to him in his adversity.

* One might suppose, from the multifarious cognominations, as the learned Doctor would style them, that this scoundrel had kept company with our Newgate birds; alias Tom, alias Jack, &c., &c.—Scratch, Nick, Beelzebub, Satan, Lucifer, &c.—See *Hudibras*, vol. ii., p. 201, *De Foe's History of the Devil*, p. 39, where he has no less than twenty-one names and titles.

† Perhaps we may be told there were no saints in heaven at that time: perhaps not; but as the *great* Milton has introduced them (see *Paradise Lost*) we may be allowed the same liberty of manufacturing nonsensical anachronisms.

‡ "Cherubim and seraphim continually cry, Holy," &c.

And after nine days arsy-versy* roll,†
Am pok'd in this damn'd black *Calcutta-hole;*
It stinks of brimstone, too—God blast it! Well,
No matter—here I shall be king of hell.‡
In hell I'll reign, then—now I know the worst;
But if I'm not revenged, may I be curst.
I'll watch Jehovah's motions day and night
And find some way to give him kick for bite:
If second best I've come off at the scratch,
Some hell-fire row I'll yet contrive to hatch,
Shall make his worship squint nine ways at once,
Or sit me down a damn'd thick-headed dunce.§

This said, he "grinned a ghastly smile," and watch'd
An opportunity, which soon he catch'd:

* "Arsy-versy—heels over head, topsy-turvy, preposterously."—*Bailey.*

† "Nine days they fell."—*Paradise Lost.* So says the *sublime* Milton. But surely this is puny fustian! It should have been nine *years* at least, to denote the vast distance of hell from heaven; though, from the gossip of Dives and Lazarus, we might suppose they were near neighbors, on the opposite side of the street; but, then, would not the heavenly choristers be annoyed with the smell of sulphur, now and then, from the den of the snake, when the wind set that way, while they were chanting hallelujah?

‡ "Better to reign in hell than serve in heaven."—*Paradise Lost.*

§ Although his cloven-footed highness here expresses himself like a blackguard (which should be overlooked, if we consider his irritated state), yet we find that he could swagger like a prince, and chatter like a prime one at other times (perhaps, as Shandy observes it was when he shook off his brimstone tunic and put on a clean shirt), when he was with his cronies (his staff-officers we may suppose)—

"To me shall be the glory sole among
Th' infernal powers in one day to have marr'd
What He (Almighty styled) six nights and days
Continued making; and who knows how long
Had been contriving!—*Paradise Lost.*

Contriving! and after all to be outwitted by the Old One! A pretty contrivance, truly! Only think, as Cobbett says, of the great Jehovah being humbugged and laughed at by such an arrant blackguard; and all, or most of the Yahoos tumbled into the dark hole, because he neglected to put on his spectacles and look sharp after the snake in the garden, or had overslept himself in his *siesta,* which we may presume he did sometimes, by his favorite *Davy's* calling so lustily to him,—"Awake, O Lord! why sleepest thou?"

For great Jehovah, it appears, thought fit
To make a world from scraps—and this is it;
This hodge-podge, hurly-burly patched-up planet,
With nothing worth a bunch of dog's meat in it,
Excepting for one highly-favored class
(For step-dame Nature sends the rest to grass);
Mixed up with odds and ends, where dry and wet,
And cold and heat, and light and dark, all meet;
Tho' at the first it looked so spruce and nice,
'Twas by the angels nicknam'd PARADISE.
And here, as in the *holy* book we read,
A YAHOO cock and hen were put to breed,
In hopes their offspring all would say their prayers,
And thus the empty benches fill up stairs,
(For Scratch had, when kick'd out in this fierce squabble,
Drawn after him a hell-fir'd gang of rabble.)
Then, to the naked, loving, Yahoo couple,
Jehovah said, " Mind, never touch an apple;
Cram if you like, from morn till night, your guts
With hips and haws, and blackberries and nuts;
But should you meddle with my Nonpareil,
By all that's good, I'll send you both to hell.
So mind your hits." For tho' in " kingdom come"
He all things knew, and dealt in FEE-FAW-FUM!
And in all common *rigs* was sharp enough,
In this *black joke* he wasn't " up to snuff."
Will all his gumption* he ne'er smelt a rat,
Or dreamt what Mister Nickibus was at;
He never guess'd what schemes the dog was brewing,
To bring his pretty Paradise to ruin;
But fagg'd, day after day, like any Turk:
When up popp'd Sooty Dun and spoil'd his work.
No sooner did *he* hear of Paradise,
Than off his rump he jump'd up in a trice;
Scrubb'd his black phiz and brimstone carcass well,
Lest he should be discovered by the smell:
Then greased his boots, and over gates and stiles,
Ere you could—sneeze, he'd stride you twenty miles;

* "Gumption, or rumgumption, comprehension, capacity."—*Cribb's Memorial.*

So eager was the dog to find out Adam;
Or, what was to his purpose more, his madam:*
Drest "a-la-mode de puppy" for this trig,
With baboon whispers, like a Bond street prig;
And was (compared with Eve's clodhopping honey)
A pretty, smirking, hell-fired Macaroni.
Now, seeing Eve in buff (for in those days
There was no laws against such *exposes*),†
It made his liqu'rish chops so run with water,
He couldn't rest a jot till he got at her;
His jawing-tackle then he ply'd so well,
She quickly nibbled at his Nonpareil.

And now a pretty mess we should be all in,
Did not the parson kindly help us out,
Owing to their confounded caterwauling;‡
But holy water makes the Devil scout.

Why didn't Adam crop the rascal's ears?
Or rather, why not snip off his bull's ——?
Then of old Scratch we should have had no fears,
Nor in his oven e'er been shov'd to frizzle?

* His madam! Yes, undoubtedly she was; and a precious, poor, soft piece of putty-like stuff the good woman seems to have been! She is first cajoled by the Old One, alias the Snake; and then goes a caterwauling with Mister Adam, without the parson's abracadabra: consequently we are all sons of a w——. See *De Foe's History of the Devil*, p. 58.

"When Beelzebub first to make mischief began,
He the woman attack'd, and she gull'd the poor man;
This Moses asserts, and from hence would infer,
That woman rules man, and the Devil rules her."

† Query—Is not the law against exposing the *person* an indirect insult against the great Jehovah, seeing he has made *the person* in his *own image* (without breeches undoubtedly)? What! ashamed of the so much boasted workmanship?

‡ "Whosoever looks back to Adam, and considers all the calamitous consequences that attended his *error*, will no longer imagine the fatal fruit to have been an apple, but the sense to be figurative. 'Tis plain that *eating* was not the crime, for we find neither the *palate* nor *mouth* of Eve punished; but when we hear '*she shall bring forth with pain*,' 'tis easy to discover the offending part."—*Swift's Discourse.*

Had not Eve munch'd the *peepin** like a jade,
No holy sprinkling we had ever needed;
But all have cried with Kecksy,† "Who's afraid?"
In short, the parson had been superseded.

Then, since these Slugs all profit so by evil,
Why try of vice the torrent so to stem?
Why should they be so spiteful to the Devil?
Were Blackey *diddled*, what becomes of them?‡

So much for Paradise, so wisely lost!
So much for Nickey, and his dingy troop!
For millions, with this rebel, down were toss'd,
And now in hell are sipping brimstone soup.

Who, that had common sense,§ could e'er believe
This silly trash of Beelzebub and Eve—
Of trees of life, and Adam, and his apple?
None with the intellects of Sancho's Dapple.
Yet this fine story, drest in pompous phrase,
Forms the first book in these *enlightened* days!‖

* Foote's Orators. † Irish Widow.

‡ "An' ye tak' awa' the Deil," says the Scotch proverb, "ye may bid gude by to the Laird." It would be a dreadful loss indeed to the black-slug tribe if Old Nick was to "kick the bucket," or be lost in a fog. There would then be wailing (but no *garnishing* of teeth) with a vengeance, and they might have recourse to "sackcloth and ashes" with propriety.

§ "Nothing," says Lord Chesterfield, "is so uncommon as common sense." Some author remarks the slowness of its growth, and says the aloe is a fool to it in comparison.

‖ Cobbett, speaking of this work, says, "The whole poem is such barbarous trash, so outrageously offensive to reason and common sense, that one is naturally led to wonder how it can have been tolerated. But it's the fashion to turn up the eyes when Paradise Lost is mentioned; and if you fail so to do, you want taste—you want judgment, even if you do not admire this absurd and ridiculous stuff."—*Register*, vol. xxxiv. p. 435. These remarks will no doubt be ascribed to Cobbett's vulgarity and defective education; but the same objection can not be made to Lord Chesterfield, who has considered Paradise Lost in nearly the same light. "I confess," says his lordship, "that I can not possibly read Milton through. Not having the honor to be acquainted with any of the parties in his poem, except the man

This childish tale affords supreme delight—
When nonsense is the bait, the gudgeons bite.
Cram ghosts and bugaboos in every tale,
To please "creation's lords" you'll never fail;*
Or give them precious holy gospel stuff,
Their maws with that can ne'er be cramm'd enough;
Naught in that *blessed* book e'er comes amiss;
Tho' old Rabshakah talks of "drinking p–ss,"†
And "eating their own dung," 'tis all divine—
Good Christian Yahoos would go there to dine.‡
'Tis only typical—dung means hot pies,
And p–ss means claret, seen with proper eyes.

and the woman, the characters and speeches of a dozen or two of angels, and of as many devils, are as much above my reach as my entertainment. Keep this secret; for if it should be known, I should be abused by every tasteless pedant and every *solid* divine in England." —*Letter* 259. *Voltaire's Candide*, chap. 25.

* "Ces sujets plaisent naturellement aux hommes: ils aiment ci qui leur parait terrible: il sont comme les enfans, qui écoutent avidement ces contes de Sorcières et de Revenants qui les effrayent. Il y a des fables pour tout âge, et il n'y a point de nation qui n'ait en les siennes. —*Essay sur la Poesie Epique.*

† "And Rabshakah said, Hath thy master sent me to thy master, and to thee, to speak these words? Hath he not sent me to the men that sit upon the wall, that they may eat their own dung and drink their own piss with you?"—Isaiah, xxxvi.

‡ And why shouldn't they? Chacun à son goût. The swinish multitude lick their gills at such holy grub, we are informed, in the eastern world, and no good reason can be assigned why they should not in the western, if they are so disposed. Why should not the contents of the close stools of the most reverend and right reverend daddies in the Lord be as sweet, relishing, and sanative, as those of the Grand Lama, and his holy crew of lickspittles? For *he* could not be supposed prolific enough to furnish *q. s.* from his own sacred *civet*-box to satisfy the ravenous maws of his loving subjects, who purchase it at an extravagant price, dried and grated, to regale with on holidays and grand festivals, when it is brought forth and considered as an exquisite delicacy and "*bonne bouche*, pour faire les viandes plus piquantes." Oh che gusto! "Apellez-vous ceci foire, bren merde, matière fécale? C'est Saphran d'Hibernia?"—*Rabelais.* See *Independent Whig*, iii., 133; *L'Espre*, 157; and *Notes to Hudibras*, ii., 304; also *Volney*, 331, and *Questions*, viii., 225, upon this very important subject.

Oh, silly biped, Rochester was right;
You shut your ears to truth, your eyes to light;
In spite of Nature's friendly admonition,
You curse yourselves, and plunge into perdition
A *four*-legg'd beast who would not rather be?
From such sophisticated reason free:
They follow all the instinct of their natures,
And are, compared with man, the wiser creatures:
They can't be made the miserable tools
Of *church* and *state*, like us, poor two-legg'd fools.*
The parson's dismal fire and brimstone tale
To *four-legg'd* cattle is of no avail.
(And no priest e'er was known so great a sot,
As go to work where nothing's to be got.)
They can not have their skulls mud-cramm'd by priests;
No hells or bugaboos will frighten beasts:
No craft can make these four-legg'd soulless things,
Fall on their knees to worship priests and kings;
The adoration kings and priests expect
Is from proud man, who boasts his intellect.

Yes, that's his boast; the slang we daily hear:
The *mind* now *marches*—like a grenadier!
Oh, glorious, wond'rous "march of intellect!"
From Yahoo brains what may we not expect?
Mind *marches* now; when thro' that it has got,
'Twill go the next stage at a gentle trot;
Then set off at a gallop, reach the goal,
And prove the Yahoo's body is all soul?
That *then* he'll be, tho' doubted heretofore,
Like Homer's vengeful hornet, "soul all o'er."†

* "Brutes find out where their talents lie:
A bear will not attempt to fly;
A founder'd horse will oft debate
Before he tries a five-barr'd gate;
A dog, by instinct, turns aside,
Whene'er he sees the ditch too wide;
But man we find the only creature,
Who, led by folly, combats Nature—
Who, when *she* loudly cries forbear,
Fixes with obstinacy there."—*Swift's Rhapsody.*

† "So burns the vengeful hornet, soul all o'er."—*Pope.*

Who'll then deny the biped's capability?
Or say he can not reach perfectibility?
Who'll *then* deny, unless they're gravel-blind,
O'er matter the omnipotence of mind?

Our great improvement now's our daily boast,
And verifies the proverb—little roast!
But do these empty boasters ever prate
Of "march of intellect" in church and state?
In these essentials what is ever done
To show us that the "mind is marching on?"
Those who contrive to keep the Yahoo blind,
Are always prating about "march of mind."
In law or gospel does it stir a peg?
Oh, no! it there has got a broken leg.
Do not the Jew-book and law jargon show,
We're what we were five hundred years ago?
The youthful mind with godly catlap fed,
Is bored with what the Lord to Moses said;
(For Moses and the Lord were very great,
And gossipped like old women *tête-a-tête;*
Till poor Lord Moses,* falling in disgrace,
Was not allow'd to see Jehovah's face;
Though still permitted his *back parts* to view,†
And cock his quizzing-glass up at his *Cue*).
The holy Bible therefore is the book
Where young and old should for instruction look.
Then hug thy "*Scripture*," Yahoo, never doubt it;
You'd tumble headlong in the PIT without it:
For though it isn't in the Ghost's handwriting,
The parsons all declare 'tis his inditing.
What inspiration glows in every line!
Aby gat Iky!—isn't that divine?
Then Iky begat Jacob; Jacob, Joe;
And Joe begat —— read Scripture, and you'll know.

* "Lord Moses," forsooth! Yes, he is so dubbed by Joshua (Numbers xi.): the *lordliness* and consequence of our right reverend prigs is therefore not so much to be wondered at.

† "And the Lord spake unto Moses face to face, as a man speaketh unto his friend, 'And thou shalt see my *back parts*, but my face shall not be seen.'"—Exod. xxxiii.—See *Clarke's Critical Review*, 37.

(No wonder they were dubb'd a "chosen nation,"
Being such dabs at holy propagation),
Of wond'rous things beside that "came to pass;"
Of kings turn'd oxen, and then turn'd to grass:*
As how a fiery cab and horses flew
From kingdom-come to fetch a conj'ring Jew!†
Of evangelic tales of cocks and bulls,
And snakes and codlings, fit for *goubemouche* gulls;
Of Noah's ark, a pious rigmarole,‡
Or, as Tim says, "A choice tale, fath and sole!"§
Then, for old women, there's a bouncing tale
Of Jonah in the belly of the whale!‖
With jaw-bone Samson, humbugg'd by his doxies,
Who fasten'd tail to tail three hundred foxes!¶

* "And Nebuchabnezzar was driven from men, and did eat grass as oxen."—Dan. iv.

† "And it came to pass, as they still went on and talked, that, behold, there appeared a chariot of fire, and horses of fire, and parted them asunder; and Elisha went up by a whirlwind into heaven."—2 Kings ii. 11.

‡ "If the Devil could but exert himself," says De Foe, "as an historian, for our improvement and diversion, what a glorious account he could give us of Noah's voyage round the world in his famous ark! He could resolve all difficulties about the building and provisioning of it for the different creatures; and also inform us whether the animals offered themselves as volunteers for the voyage, or whether he went a hunting for them," &c.—*History of the Devil.*

§ Foote's "Knights."

‖ "And Jonah was in the belly of the whale three days and three nights." "The great fish that swallowed up Jonah, surrendered him again without hurting a hair of his head, or even charging him anything for his three days' lodging."—*New Monthly Mag.*

"Then, for a pretty Bible tale,
Haven't you one about a whale
That swallow'd Jonah? though the Jew
Had such rank flesh, he made him spew."
Homer Burlesqued.

¶ "And Samson said, With the jaw-bone of an ass have I slain a thousand men." This was certainly pretty good smiting, especially for a lord judge. No wonder he was weary and thirsty, since, at the rate of one a minute (and allowing the Philistines to have had paper skulls, it could not have been well done in less time), it would have required seventeen hours to get through the job, without any time for

Poor Jerry's "old cast clouts" and "naughty figs;"*
Elisha's bears;† the Devil and the Pigs;‡
A talking jackass, next—blind Balaam's Neddy,§
Who to the prophet's thwacks replied so ready:
Then, for quack-doctors what a charming prize,
There's clay and spittle salve to cure sore eyes!‖
Lot's rib of salt, with his two brimstone jades,

rest and refreshment! But what a dab at fox-hunting this lord judge must have been to catch three hundred, and then tie them tail to tail, that they might run the better! No wonder that such a lord judge was *diddled* by *Dally*.

* "And he said unto Jeremiah, Put these old cast clouts and rotten rags under thine arm holes," &c.—"One basket had very good figs, and the other basket had very *naughty* figs."—Jer. xxxviii.

† "And there came forth little children, and mocked him, and said, Go up thou bald head! And Elisha cursed them in the name of the Lord" (one should have thought it was in the name of the Devil); and there came two she-bears out of the wood, and tare forty and two children of them."—2 Kings ii.

A proper punishment for snotty brats, who called the Lord's conjuror bald-pate!" But what a crusty cock of a prophet! Didn't he know that of such was the kingdom of heaven? Though perhaps they may learn better manners when they are there, otherwise they might have called him *bald-pate* again when they met with him in the upper gallery, where we may presume he could have found no *she-bears* to *tare* them.

‡ "Then went the devils out of the man, and entered into the swine." We are not informed (which is much to be regretted) at which door front or back, these devils trotted into the pigs' apartments, though it is most likely it was at the postern gate, as they were hardly such spooneys as to run the risk of being guillotined by trying for admission at the *snout* door; besides, they could so much easier slip out at the *back* door, when they were surfeited with chitterlings and pigs' fry, and bilk their landlords.

§ "And Balaam's anger was kindled, and he smote the ass with a staff; and the Lord opened the mouth of the ass, and she said unto Balaam, What have I done unto thee that thou hast smitten me? and Balaam said unto the ass, Because thou hast mocked me. And the ass said unto Balaam, Am I not thine ass?" What a holy and edifying confab! It is a pity the Lord does not open the jaws of the poor animals at present, that they might threaten the brutal Christian *Yahoo* drivers with the "wrath to come" for their infernal cruelty.

‖ "And he spat on the ground and made clay of the spittle, and he anointed the eyes of the blind man with the clay."—John ix.

Who were so terrified at being maids*
They made their old dad groggy—how sublime!
Children should read such godly books in time.
Oh, blessed Scripture! what a heavenly treasure
For those who read and can reflect at leisure!
What squabbling tribes of "*tites*, and *ites*, and *bites!*"
Uzzites, Hittites, Moabites, and Gir-go-shites?
How edifying! Then, what chaste discourses
Of ladies who, for sweethearts, talk of horses!†
Oh, shame, where is thy blush? Here's godly reading,
To teach young girls at boarding-school good *breeding!*‡
(From whence sent to their *Ma's*, accomplished quite,
They read the "word of God" on Sunday night;)
Zekiel's *bonne-bouche*, too! which the dainty Jew
Turn'd up his nose at, saying he should sp—;§
Why couldn't this old Tyke have lunch'd in quiet,

* "And Lot's wife looked back, and she became a pillar of salt."—Gen. xix. Saint Irenæus (what saints!) says, the wife of Lot remains "dans le pays de Sodome, non plus en chair corruptible, mais en statue de sel permanent, et montrant par ses parties naturelles les effets ordinaires." Tertullian (another of the gabbling gang called *Fathers of the Church*), in his poem on this very delicate and important subject, says,

"Diciturat vivens alio sub corpore sexus
Mirifice solito dispungere sanguine menses."

Doctor South has observed, in speaking of the Apocalypse, that if it did not find the reader mad, it always left him so; but may not the same be said, with great truth, of the whole bundle of inspired trash, which fills half the mad-houses of Europe!

† "For she doated upon their paramours, whose flesh is as the flesh of asses, and whose issue is like the issue of horses."—Ezek. xxiii.

‡ See the pompous prospectus of Mrs. Grant's establishment at Park-house, Croydon; in which Mrs. G. observes (among other frothy stuff) that "the church and scriptural catechisms, with the *records* of the Holy Bible, are deeply impressed on the tender minds of the young ladies committed to her care, by constant study and written exercises."

§ "And thou shalt *eat* it as barley cakes, and thou shalt *bake* it with dung that cometh out of man in their sight. Then said I, Ah, Lord God! behold my soul hath not been polluted."—Ezek. iv. We may observe, that, owing no doubt to the extreme *delicacy* of the translators, the word *bake* is substituted for *eat*. The original, or at least the Latin text, is, "placentem autem hordei quam *comedes* ipsam stereoribus excrementi humani, parato in occulis illorum."

Said grace, and lick'd his gills, for such choice diet?
Then Davy, how superlatively good!
Who wished to wash his petticoats in blood!
And that the bow-wows running in the street
Might lick the blood from off his holy feet!*
Blest Davy, "after God's own heart," the man!
Who put Uriah in the battle's van,
And got his rib;† but this displeased the Lord,
Who by the parish conjuror sent him word,
That on the *house-top* his seraglio
Should with his neighbor be a public show,
Before all Israel, and before the sun;
(Which, no doubt, caused the old-clothes mob much fun).
A prophet, next, comes tramping through the streets,‡
Bare-buttock'd, telling all the girls he meets
That he had been with child, and brought forth wind,§
Which sounded like a harp (perhaps behind);‖
And that if ladies rigg'd themselves so fine,
And put rings in their snouts, like filthy swine,
The Lord would smite them all with scabby nobs,
And what's more shocking show their THINGUMBOBS.¶

* "That thy foot may be dipped in the blood of thine enemies, and the tongue of thy dogs in the same."—Psalm lxviii.

† "Thus saith the Lord, I will take thy wives before thine eyes, and give them to thy neighbor, and he shall lie with thy wives in the sight of the sun; for thou didst it secretly, but I will do *this thing* before all Israel, and before the sun! [Pretty stuff for the Lord to jabber about!] So they spread Absalom a tent upon the top of the house, and Absalom went in [how delicate] unto his father's concubines, in the sight of *all* Israel." Only *ten* ladies! Bravo, little Aby! No wonder his dad fretted after him so, when he was caught by his ragged locks to the tree. In the prophesy, his *neighbor* was to lie with his wives; it is fulfilled by his *son* lying with his concubines. Mais c'est égal—it's all holy in the eyes of the Bible-grubbers. A t—'s as good for a sow as a pancake.—See *Clarke's Review.*

‡ "And the Lord said, Like as my servant Isaiah hath walked naked and barefoot three years, &c., so shall the king of Assyria lead away the Egyptian prisoners and captives, young and old, *naked* and barefoot, even with their *buttocks* uncovered."—Isaiah xx.

§ "We have been with child, we have been in pain, we have as it were brought forth wind."—Isaiah xxvi.

‖ "Wherefore my bowels shall sound like an harp."—Isaiah xvi.

¶ "Moreover, the Lord saith, Because the daughters of Zion are

Such is the Christian Yahoo's holy treasure,
Which yields knaves profit, and gives idiots pleasure!
Since Holy Bible reading is the taste,
No wonder all our females are so chaste.
Can ribaldry like this be edifying,
So full of smiting, smuttiness, and lying?
What holy hogwash for a chosen nation!
Is such a book the turnpike to salvation?
Can such disgusting stuff be deemed "God's word?"
Or such humgruffians favorites with the Lord?
Such filthy cannibals, who hadn't sense
To hide their UNCLEAN THINGS, which gave offence;
Till Moses bid them dig a hole and hide 'em,*
Because the Lord, he said, could not abide 'em;
And didn't wish, while lounging in their tents,
To be regaled with such ambrosial scents:
For where such lolypops were strew'd about,
It smelt like *modern Athens* there's no doubt.
Oh, Moses, Moses! wherefore, Mister Moses,
Didst thou not in their tansies rub their noses?
Since nasty curs, the connoisseurs all say,
If you repeat the dose, are cured that way.
Thou shouldst have served such stinkards puppy fashion,†
For putting *Goramity* in a passion.
No wonder, worried by such unlick'd bears,
The Lord so often like a trooper swears.‡

haughty, and walk with stretched forth necks and wanton eyes, walking and mincing as they go: therefore the Lord will smite with a SCAB the crown of the head of the daughters of Zion, and the Lord will discover their SECRET PARTS; and the Lord will take away their rings and their *nose*-jewels; and instead of a sweet smell there shall be a stink."—Isaiah iii.

* "And thou shalt have a paddle upon thy weapon, and it shall be when thou wilt *ease* thyself abroad, thou shalt dig therewith, and shalt turn back and cover (very cleanly!) *that* which cometh from thee."—Exodus xxxii. "For the Lord thy God walketh in the midst of thy camp; therefore shalt thy camp be holy, that he see no UNCLEAN THING in thee, and turn away from thee."—Deut. xxiii.

† St John the Divine differs in opinion with Mister Moses; since he says (Rev. xxii.), "He that is filthy let him be filthy still."

‡ "How long will this people provoke me?"—Numb. xiv. "Unto whom I sware in my wrath," &c.

Angelic Yahoo! though thy form's divine,*
Thy intellect denotes thee but a swine:
Cajoled and fleeced by church and state combin'd,
Yet proudly prating of thy "march of mind!"
If trash like this can for religion pass,
Cudgell'd and kicked thou shouldst be for an ass.

But though the Yahoo with this Bible stuff
Is to the gullet cramm'd, 'tis not enough
To stifle reason; and to garble truth,
A vampire tribe beset him from his youth;
Well knowing if they could but keep him blind,
They could no longer holy plunder find:
Hence youth are pestered morning, noon, and eve,
With '*chart* in heaven,† *grace*, and "*I believe*;"‡
Then, lest the head should be from lumber freed,
'Tis bother'd with an Athanasian Creed;
Hymns, tracts, and liturgies, complete the twaddle,
And leave the Yahoo a well furnished noddle.

But Law contributes, law may claim a share

* "In action how like an angel."—*Hamlet.*

† "'*Chart* in heaven," is the gabble of children morning and evening; and snuffled over with their "*Ibleve*," or "*Suffry dunder*," to the great edification of the brats, and delight of their parents, who would be horrified if this unmeaning stuff was once neglected. The grace is snuffled over, that the Lord may *sanctify* the *prog* for their use, and themselves to the Lord's *sarvice*. (What the Devil *sarvice* can they render the Lord? But why is this mummery omitted at breakfast and tea? Are those refreshmeuts not worth thanking the Lord for? And why is not grace said, upon certain occasions, at bed-time? Surely, says Voltaire, "une belle femme vaut bein un souper!" And to beg of the Lord to "sanctify these *creatures* to our use," would be a very rational and appropriate petition at such times.

‡ Few governments wish for enlightened subjects. "Train up a child in the way he should go;" *i. e.*, brutalize him in order to render him abject and subservient, and then upbraid him with his brutality. Tie a tin kettle to a dog's tail, and set up the cry of mad-dog, and he will soon get his brains knocked out. Priests, from their supposed sanctity, have unfortunately acquired such an ascendency in society, that they may be considered as the principal springs and levers in all governments. "Church and state" is the general cry (church first, as the most influential); and it has ever been the grand undeviating maxim of the church to "train up a child in the way he should go."

In making *godlike* Yahoos what they are.*
They law and church together are combined,
And trot on, cheek by jowl, the rest to blind.
For CHURCH and STATE bawls every *learned brother*,
And one grand humbug countenances t'other.
For right or wrong, they plead with equal glee,
" C'est tout égal," their object is the Fee.
In all the mummery of gown and wig,
See on the bench an antiquated prig;
How like a wond'rous oracle he prates,
Directing Gotham jury's addled pates;
Quotes Coke and Hale, and Littleton and Selden,†
(All wonders in their day like our great Eldon)
Who framed wise laws to check the horrid evil
Of being " instigated by the devil."‡
Oh! what wise ancestors! what legislators.
Dame Nature surely meant them for bull-baiters.
Laws upon laws against imagined crimes;
As well adapted to " enlightened" times!
Their grave import each learned blockhead feels,
By deodands on horses and cart-wheels.§

* It appears as if the *Lamb*, alias the blessed Redeemer, had conceived a very unfavorable opinion of the latitat tribe (who, it is very *possible*, were in his time but a shabby set), or he would not have expressed himself with such bitterness in speaking of them: for example, "And he said, Woe unto you also, ye lawyers! for ye lade men with burdens grievous to be borne, and ye yourselves touch not the burdens with one of your fingers. Woe unto you, lawyers! for ye have taken away the key of knowledge."—Luke x. 46, 52.

† In the present so much boasted age of " intellect," we hear these authorities quoted as prodigies of wisdom and excellence; yet this *great* Sir Matthew Hale condemned several poor old women to the gallows for witchcraft.

‡ The ridiculous fudge from our enlightened ancestors, in the preamble to all criminal indictments, and still kept up as an illustration of the *spread*.

§ "Deodand (deodandum) a thing devoted to God for expiation of his wrath, or to atone for the violent death of a man by misadventure."—*Bailey*. Jacob's Law Dictionary says, "given or rather forfeited to God for the pacification of his wrath." Is it any wonder our venerable ancestors are so highly extolled? A poor old woman being deaf, or perhaps drunk, is run over by a cart, when the *wheel* is given to the great Jehovah to appease his wrath! What has provoked his wrath? Oh, divine Yahoo! "In apprehension how like a god!"

Ordeals, magic, laws for hanging witches,*
And throwing women into ponds and ditches!
For it was soon discovered by their swimming,
Whether they witches were, or mere old women.
Then searching them for private teats, to show
Whether they suckled Beelzebub or no!†
Wager of battle laws! and some (what sport!)
Sent ladies riding on a ram in court!‡
Stick-chopping sheriffs proving themselves able;
And lord mayors counting hobnails on a table!§

* By the express command of the holy bugaboo, Exod. xxii. 18, and Lev. xx. 27, wizards and witches are to be put to death; and upon this *holy* authority the British Solomon founded his Demonology, of which the following is an extract:—

Question. "What forme of punyshment thinke ye merites magiciens and witches?"

King. "They ought to be put to dethe, according to the law of God."

Question. "But what kynde of dethe I pray you?"

King. "It is commonly by fyre."

Question. "But ought no sex, age, nor rank to be excused?"

King. "None at all ——."

So much for the wisdom and humanity of this precious Lord's anointed; no wonder he has been held up as a prodigy by the clergy, who have always profited by the ignorance and barbarity of the people, and who will sanction and justify from holy writ, the continuance of such atrocities in the remote parts of the country, as far as they are able. This *royal pitoyable*, in the conference at Hampton Court, jabbered so much to the purpose, that Archbishop Whitgift (who, as Lord Bolingbroke observes, died soon after, and most probably doated then), declared that "verily the king spake by the spirit of God." It appears from some letters in the Harlein MSS. that *Jammie* had a thick skull. "They could hardly," says the letter to Sir Wm. Hollende, "breake it open with a chisel and a saw, and so full of brains, as they could not, upon the opening, keep them from splitting; a great proof of his infinite judgment."—*Relics of Literature*, 226. See Bishop Jewell's vehement admonition to Queen Elizabeth to prosecute witches and sorcerers with severity, from which, and other similar remonstrances, by the church gang, witchcraft and enchantment were made felony soon after; and in the year 1612, nineteen poor wretches were tried at Lancaster for witchcraft, ten of whom were condemned and executed.

† It was the usual practice to strip the poor women for this purpose, and also to prick them with pins, or scratch them with brambles, to see if they would bleed.

‡ See this explained in Bailey's Dictionary, word *Free-bench.*

§ See an excellent burlesque on the wise laws and customs of our ancestors in Goldsmith's 13th essay.

Such were our great grand-dads! what a breed!
From whom our great mind-marching race proceed.
No wonder Yahoos boast their genealogy,
Or rave about the humbug of phrenology;
By which great doctors (Splitskull, Fudge, and Co.),
From bumps upon the nob can plainly show
Whether the boy will be a thief or no.
For if nobs on the sconce so guide the mind,
The fingers will to pilfering be inclined;
Thus destined to the *drop* he can not shun it,
The cursed bumps upon his nob have done it.

Oh, intellect! how far and wide's thy *spread*,
Fermenting in each lubber's loggerhead.
Not only is it shown on skulls by bumps,
But also in fool's tricks, hops, skips, and jumps!
All hail, gymnastics! (ass tricks) what a sight!
Boys walking on their heads, their heels upright!
What joy to see his sons, the parent feels,
Bending sea-crabs, and turning Cath'rine wheels.
Will climbing ladders backward, leaping ditches,
And playing such fool's antics bring in riches?
A money-getting itch 'tis, no doubt, stirs 'em;
Oh, brilliant trio! Voelker, Gall, and Spurzheim!
While each one for a prodigy now passes,
Who'd ever think of "writing them down asses?"*
Their sapient followers, one and all, indeed,
Might be set down, with truth, of long-ear'd breed.

Hail, glorious age! when science so abounds,
That our sea-captains give a dozen pounds
To purchase a child's caul, as then they know
They can't to Davy Jones's locker go.†

* "Oh, that he were but here to write me down an ass."—*Shakspere.*

† Another striking proof of the *march!* In the most respectable journals, advertisements are every day inserted announcing children's *cauls* for sale at from £10 to £20 each; which were purchased by captains of ships as sure preservatives against drowning! Bits of scarlet rags are also bought by the same wiseacres, chiefly Greenland captains, of old women, supposed witches in Norway, for the purpose of procuring favorable winds in returning home

And when in Norway, seek for some old hag,
Of whom they buy a slip of scarlet rag;
Which, being fastened to the vessel's masts,
Saves the sea-lubbers from all adverse blasts.

But there's the stage! does that co-operate,
And furnish lumber for the Yahoo's pate?
Oh, yes! the theatre itself is made
A kind of hot-bed for the humbug trade!
When ghosts and goblins are personified,
The audience, one and all, are horrified;
The "ad captandam vulgus" is a ghost,
Which touches Yahoo's tender feelings most;
For tho' such grim hobgoblins yield delight,
They at the same time cause a dreadful fright,*
And strike with terror, more than pulpit prosing,
Which lulls the congregation oft to dozing;
Hence parsons all, of every age and size,
Are ever puffing Shakspere to the skies;
Convinced his pale-faced ghosts with bloody sconces,
Will cause most terror to priest-ridden dunces.
Hence Shakspere mania, every dolt can quote,
From his puff'd plays, whole sentences by rote:
While those who hear the ranting, at each line,
Cry out, "How charming!" "Oh, that's very fine!"

Nor less delighted are the Yahoo rabble,
To hear the witches round the kettle gabble,†

* "How odd a single hobgoblin's nonentity,
Should cause more fear than a whole host's identity."
Byron.

† Could any one suppose an audience, boasting their rationality, could sit to hear, much more to take delight in, such disgusting gibberish, hardly fit for a Bartlemy fair mob.

Very few writers, excepting Rymer and Cobbett, have ventured to point out the absurdities of the *divine* bard, which indeed is considered as petty treason; the latter, however, speaks out boldly. "After his ghosts, witches, sorcerers, fairies, and monsters; after his bombast, and puns, and smut, what is it can make a nation admire Shakspere? What is it that can make them call him a divine bard, nine-tenths of whose works are made up of such trash as any decent man would be ashamed to put his name to? The time will undoubtedly come, when the whole of this stuff will, by the natural good sense of the nation, be consigned to everlasting oblivion."—*Register*, vol. 34, p. 435.

Of mixing toad and blood of bat together
Wih grease scrap'd from the gallows in hot weather,
And putting in, with other filth to stew,
"Turk's nose, frog's toes, and liver of a Jew."
Then stirring it nine times to brew up trouble,
Or in their jargon, "make the hell-broth bubble."
Is it a wonder hags and ghosts affright,
When such bombast is spouted every night?*
Then while the hags sink down before his eyes,
To see Macbeth gape up toward the skies,
And give amidst his "start, and stare, and stagger,"†
A flying leap to catch the "air-drawn dagger!"
But Banquo's ghost's the thing, when pale as death,
He up the trap-door pops to scare Macbeth;
With visage grim, and stiff about the crupper,
He squats down with the quality to supper:
While they with wonder at each other stare,
To hear such ranting at an empty chair:
He's raving at the ghost (which they don't see),
And cries, "Don't shake your gory locks at me."

Since superstition rules the YAHOO most,
There's nothing for the parson like a ghost;‡
While he can keep his noodles in a fright,
With ghosts and devils, all will go on right.
Is it a wonder, then, that such a scribe
Should be a fav'rite with the humbug tribe?

That Shakspere copied Nature is the cry;
But Nature may be copied in her sty:

* See Beauchamp's excellent Analysis, 192.

† "And strut, and storm, and straddle, stamp and stare."—A line in Cowper's *Task*, describing players.

‡ Every person endeavors to inculcate a belief in ghosts and witches, as tending to perpetuate fear and ignorance, their grand and only supporters. Crabbe confesses their utility, and classes unbelievers with ruffians in the true spirit of Christian charity.

"Each village inn has heard the ruffian boast,
That he believ'd in neither God nor Ghost."—*Parish Register.*

All which is riveted by the blessed Jew book, where Samuel's ghost is adverted to as a knock you down argument, if you demur.

As Voltaire once remark'd by his *derriere*,
Which, though 'twas Nature, he wrapt up with care.

Does Nature prompt Othello's blackguard roar—*
"Villain, be sure you prove my wife a whore!"†
To murder Desdemona, and then tell,
In language Billingsgate can not excel,
"She's like a liar gone to burn in hell!"
And can such ribaldry, such vulgar stuff
Give pleasure? yes, 'tis Shakspere's—that's enough;
To find fault with *his* plays is petty treason;
We must not bring them to the test of reason:
They're meant, like other precious stuff, for cramming in
The Yahoo's empty pate without examining.

Who'd sit to hear such trash as Cymbeline,
Were it not Shakspere's? *then* its very fine!
How poor Iachimo must sweat and fume,
Coop'd in his box, while in the lady's room!

* See the excellent remarks upon this Blackamoor's rant in Rymer's "Short View of Tragedy," and also on the absurdities of Shakspere's *Julius Cæsar*.

† The following lines are in part extracted from the Epilogue to the Clandestine Marriage. A party, after quitting the card table, begin discoursing on the plays of Shakspere:—

Sir Pat'k Mahoney. "King Lare's touching! and how fine to see
Ould Hamlet's ghost! To be or not to be
What are your op'ras to Othello's roar?
Oh, he's an angel of a blackamoor!
Lord Minum. What, when he chokes his wife?
Col. Trill. And calls her whore?
Sir Pat. King Richard calls his horse,—and then Macbeth,
Who talks of murder till he's out of breath!
My blood runs cowld at every syllable;
Lord Min. And then he spies a dagger—
Col. Trill. That's invisible!
Sir Pat. Oh, botheration! how could he suppose
A bloody dagger dangled at his nose?
And jump to catch it!
Col. Trill. Had it been a dagger
He might have cut his thumb!
Lord Min. And spoil'd his swagger."
[*All laugh.*

See an excellent burlesque of this Tom-a-Bedlam foolery in the "Rejected Addresses."

Suppose, while button'd up for this strange frolic,
He had been troubled with the windy colic!
How the poor lady in her bed must funk
At hearing loud explosions in the trunk!

Next Shylock comes, a cannibal old Jew,
Who claims a pound of flesh, by bond his due.
No words his savage rancor can assuage,
He brings his weights and scales upon the stage;
Then whets his knife to cut it in the sight
Of Christian Yahoos, to their great delight.*

Behold King Lear, who raves in his oration,
For musk to sweeten his imagination.†
Why, what has tainted it? the reader cries;
Ask ladies, who praise Shakspere to the skies.

See Hamlet's hair (or wig) stand bolt upright,‡
Like quills upon the porcupine, with fright;
His daddy's ghost comes all in armor drest—
(A queer ghost's jacket it must be confess'd):
"Angels," he cries, "and ministers of grace,"
In horror at the phantom's powder'd face:
But when the bugaboo down stairs has got,
He cracks his jokes with it—his fright's forgot;
And while the spectre underground cries "Swear!"
Says, "Ha! old Truepenny, what, art thou there?"

* How such horrible and disgusting stuff can be delighted in is astonishing! It serves, however, to keep up animosity, and exasperate one class of citizens against another, by which they are all more easily managed and kept in subjection. Divide and conquer is the grand *sine qua non* of all governments.

† "Down from the waist they are centaurs, tho' women all above; but to the girdle do the gods inherit, beneath is all the fiends. There's hell—there's darkness—there is the sulphurous pit, burning, scalding, stench, consumption: fie, fie, fie: pah, pah: give me an ounce of civet, good apothecary, to sweeten my imagination!" There's a neat, genteel speech for royalty to spout.

‡ The tragedy performers in Pope's time wore enormous Caxons; Cibber tells us his *jasey* cost him forty guineas!

"——— what made the people stare?
Cato's great wig."

These are rough sketches of our fav'rite plays,
That yield such raptures, and obtain such praise:
From such choice specimens of Shakspere's pages,
Is it a wonder Shakspere-mania rages?
Such fustian hodge-podge, hatch'd from childish tales,
Where ghosts and hags, and mummery prevails,
Are well adapted for a Yorkshire fair,
To make clodhopping bumpkins grin and stare:
But in this boasted *intellectual* age,
To bring such trumpery upon the stage;
In London, too, the seat of art and science,
To set all common sense so at defiance!
To puff "th' immortal bard" up to the sky,*
Shows YAHOOS are but babes, tho' six feet high;
And that 'tis raree-shows they most delight in,
With Punch and Judy and the Devil fighting.

Survey the biped race in ev'ry state,
The rich, the poor, the vulgar, and the great;
In what class or condition can we trace,
The "little less than angel" in the race?†

* No manufacturer of bombast, or rattle bladder trash, has ever been so wonderfully *puffed* up or extolled as Shakspere. But as poor Sancho observes, "There's never a why but there's a wherefore." By the vampire tribe he is held up as a prodigy, from the great service he has rendered them by his personifications of ghosts and phantoms; and by the YAHOOS in general, from his having beplastered them so *neatly!* "Caw me, caw thee;" but *hear him*, as they cry in a certain kennel, when any honorable gentleman is speaking nonsense.

"What a piece of work is man! how noble in reason! [Is not this ironical? *Reason*, and whitewashing with *lamb's blood*, do not well assimilate.] How infinite in faculties; in form and moving how express and admirable; in action how like a god! the beauty of the world; the paragon of animals!" Bravo, the divine bard. He does the thing handsomely, and dabs it on pretty thick, but it all sticks. The Yahoo's vanity has stomach for it all. No wonder, after such a luscious lollypop they should dub him divine, and so incessantly bellow forth his wonderful knowledge of human nature. Blarney for ever!

† It is much to be regretted that Pope has not explained to us what angels were. It would have amused us to know how they spend their time when they have done singing and trumpeting; whether they fly about with their goose wings stuck on their shoulders, what are their wants, and how they are gratified; whether they eat and drink, &c.; and whether, if they do, it all transpires in ambrosial perspiration; or whether there's a necessity for a "wha wants me?"—See *Martinus Scriblerus*, chap. 7.

But what are angels? lubbers with goose wings!
What nonsense a great poet sometimes sings.

See the poor sailor dragg'd out like a dog,
To murder, or be murdered for king Log.*
On board a floating-hell he's hauled to fight,†
And neither knows nor cares who's wrong or right:‡
He takes his quid and grog, and damns his eyes,
Till by a chain-shot cut in two he dies.
Or see the martial hero glory seek,
Urg'd on by fame and eighteen-pence a week:§

* "I own," says Chesterfield to his son, "that I have a great regard for king Log."

† Black floating hells was the name given by the Americans to our men-of-war, during the Revolution,—in which they so happily succeeded.

‡ Copenhagen and Navarino, for example.

§ "Ou trouver des hommes qui pour 5 ou 6 sous par jour affrontent dans les combats, la mort, ou les maladies, s'ils avoient le sens commun." The pay of the Russian cut-throats is about 2s. 6d. per month. —See *Erasme de la Folie*, p 45.

"One to destroy is murder by the law,
And gibbets keep the lifted hand in awe;
To murder thousands takes a specious name,
War's *glorious* art, and gives immortal fame."—*Young.*

For a true history of the Yahoo in all his brilliancy and *godlike* heroism, the reaper is referred to the description of the battle between the two frigates, in Lieutenant Smith's "Sailors and Saints," where he is is delineated in the full indulgence of his butchering propensity, covered with gore and *glory*. Surely the Yahoo must smell of blood in the next world, if he is not well scoured with the soap-suds of regeneration, and purified by the "new birth unto righteousness." What can the Devil want such bloodhounds for?" *Mais taisez-vous*—they're *jolly tars.*

"The cunning of mankind," says Arbuthnot, "never exerts itself so much as in their arts of destroying one another."—See *Swift's Brobdignag*, chap. 7, where their ingenuity in this particular is well described.

"Les plus *honnetes* gens apprirent à compter parmi leurs devoirs celui d'égorger leurs semblables; on vit les hommes se massacrer par milliers sans savoir pourquoi."—*Rousseau.*

"For soldiers, if they thought aright,
Would all as soon be damn'd as fight
For kings, who, when they've lost a leg,
Will hardly give 'em leave to beg."—*Homer Burlesqued.*

With colors flying they all march in order,
Told by the parson "killing is no murder."
Thousands of strutting *godlike* Yahoo heroes
March out to fight, to please two royal Neros;
Who wallow in their styes, while these train'd brutes
Are sacrificed to settle their disputes;
And when one half are killed, the other boasts
How much they're succor'd by the "Lord of Hosts."
One side Te-deums sings, and so does t'other;*
The Lord has help'd king Log, and king Log's brother.†
"God's images" by thousands are at once
Kill'd off‡ to please a "Lord's anointed" dunce!
A dunce anointed! Can legitimates
Have, like their stupid subjects, wooden pates?
Yes; blocks alike, they're tutored all by priests;§
The only diff'rence is, they're *royal* beasts:
Their skulls are stuffed the same with fee-faw-fum,
With hocus-pocus,|| hell, and kingdom-come.

But still such monarchs, tho' with wooden nobs,
Are suited best to wooden-headed mobs,¶

* "That like the Briton and the Gaul,
Both sides may sing, and roar, and bawl,
Te Deum, tho' for nought at all;
And tell the Lord a cursed lie,
That both have got the victory."—*Homer Burlesqued.*

† In all epistolary correspondence between the Lord's anointed, they always subscribe themselves *royal brothers.*

‡ "Killed off" was the usual laconic unfeeling answer of Mr. Windham, then secretary-at-war, when questioned as to the great deficiencies in the returned skeleton regiments from America. A proof how heroes are appreciated when they can no longer stand to be shot at.

§ "Malheur aux nations qui confient l'éducation de leur citoyens aux prêtres," says Helvetius. "Beaucoup mieux vaudroit ne leur en donner aucune." To which may be added the observation of Goldsmith—"The countries where sacerdotal instruction alone is permitted, remain in ignorance, superstition, and slavery."

|| A corruption of "hoc est corpus meum," a part of the sacrament gabble: for the consolation of idiots, alias Christians, who make no doubt of being hugged in Abraham's bosom if they chew a bit of the Lord's body, by way of quid, to comfort themselves with, as they jog along from "this ere world to that ere."

¶ "How goes the mob? (for that's a mighty thing),
When the king's trump the mob are for the king."—*Dryden.*

Who roar and stretch their ell-wide jaws, and sing
For any royal dolt, "God save the king!"*
It matters not, tho' made of rotten stuff,
If he's the "Lord's anointed," that's enough.†
A jackass, 'dizen'd out in robes of state,
Let an archbishop but anoint his pate,
And dub him sacred, soon would be ador'd—
The YAHOO mob would hail him "sovereign lord:"
Most humbly they'd profess themselves to be
The vassals of his GRACIOUS majesty;‡
A lubber only fit the crows to scare,
Or carry guts to feed a hungry bear:
Clap but a tinsel bauble on his sconce,
His imperfections vanish all at once;§
He's God's viceregent, and by right divine
Can at his pleasure flog his herd of swine.

The Jews, we're by the Lord's lieutenant told,‖
Worshipp'd a calf, that Aaron made, of gold;¶

* "Well, if the king's a lion, at the least,
The people are a many-headed beast."—*Pope.*

† "What the Lord sends us surely must be good,
Although 'tis but a piece of rotten wood."—*Pindar.*

‡ If any one of these sacred noodles vouchsafed to open his royal mouth, whatever he utters must be *gracious*, forsooth! Yes, most gracious, although it should be a recommendation to a gang of parasites to strip the last shirt from off the backs, and the last penny from the pockets of his loving, swinish subjects, to enable gingerbread-gilt trumpeters to wear laced jackets at £70 a piece! Is there neither shame nor common sense anywhere but in America?

§ "Prendi uom rozzo e comun, fanne un monarca,
Tosto il favor del ciel sopra gli piove;
Tosto divien di sapienza un'arca;
Nella testa di lui s'alloggia Giove:
Decide, ordina, giudica: un oracolo
Tutto a un tratto divien: pare un miracolo."—*Casti.*

‖ Moses is so designated by Hobbes.

¶ "And I said unto them, whosoever hath any gold, let them break it off; so they gave it me: then I cast it into the fire, and there came out this calf."—Exod. xxxii. "And he [Moses] said unto them, Put every man his sword by his side, and go through the camp, and slay every man his brother, and every man his companion. And they did

For which, as in the holy book 'tis written,
Three thousand of the snipcock race were smitten,
While Aaron 'scap'd! Just as in modern times,
The great remain unpunish'd for their crimes.*
But do not Christian Yahoos every day
To golden calves their adoration pay?†
The gin-drench'd rabble always will adore
The titled, lordly crew, who keep them poor:‡
With equal admiration they all stare
At Spain's doll-dresser,§ or a Russian bear;
Or hug a filthy, stinking Cossack,‖ rot 'em,
And run to hell to kiss a ROYAL bottom.¶

so according to the word of Moses; and there fell of the people that day about 3,000 men."—Ibid.

"And the Lord plagued the people, because *they made* the calf which Aaron made."—Ibid. This is as clear as mud; but the ghost in many instances, seemed a thick-skulled one at inditing.

* "Small rogues in hempen ropes oft swing,
While great ones gain a red silk string:
The trade is learn'd in half an hour,
To spare the rich and flog the poor."—*Homer Burlesqued.*

† "Fools that we are, like Israel's fools of yore,
The calf ourselves have fashion'd we adore:
But should true reason once resume her reign,
The god will dwindle to a calf again."—*Churchill.*

‡ "The dustman in his cart that hourly slaves,
Drawn by an ass, the partner of his toils,
Is far superior to such titled knaves,
In coaches glitt'ring with a nation's spoils."—*Pindar.*

§ This truly *pitoyable* "Lord's anointed" amused himself, during his captivity in France, in working muslin petticoats for a wooden doll, called the Virgin Mary! A specimen of royal intellect.

‖ The savage who came to exhibit himself after Bonaparte's defeat in Russia, when thousands went to gape at him in Hyde Park, and other public places, as a prodigy.

¶ "E quei: fu giusto ognor creduto e detto,
Che il suddito al sovran la zampa lecchi
Di dipendenza in segno e di rispetto;
Ma se la zampa a far leccar ti secchi,
Farti altre parti anche leccar tu puoi:
Tutti ti leccheran quel che tu vuoi."—*Casti.*

Whoe'er would witness folly's highest sport,
Let him behold a collar-day at court:*
Whoe'er would see Tom-fools, may here find plenty;
For one they'll see elsewhere, they'll here find twenty.
See "king-at-arms," in all their buckram state!
What stars and ribands on the childish great!†
What illustrissimos and excellencies!
Hung round with colored strings, to please their fancies!
What lacquer'd puppets! what a raree-show!‡
Are these the "Tiddydolls" to whom we bow?
See Lady Squab among the doll-drest group!
Is that a YAHOO with that monstrous hoop?
The upper half preserves the likeness still,
The lower has been thro' the flatting-mill.
Use reconciles us to such uncouth shapes,
Or we should laugh to see such human apes.
What starch-phizz'd poker-back'd, fine dukes and lords!
Lisping their pretty namby-pamby words!
This nincompoop's dubb'd royal—*that* serene;§
But what does such slop-dawdle nonsense mean?
How do these lordships, highnesses, and graces,
Refrain from laughing in each other's faces?

* A collar-day is a festival when the knights wear their collars of SS. round their necks as ornaments.—*Bailey.*

† "L'opinion et le préjugé viennent à bout de faire passer pour une decoration honorable, les signes les plus puériles, et les plus ridicules." —*Du Marsais.*

‡ "You must renounce courts," says Lord Chesterfield, "if you will not connive at knaves and tolerate fools; their number makes them considerable."

"But how, my muse, canst thou refuse so long,
The bright temptation of the courtly throng?
The most inviting theme:—the court affords
Much food for satire; it abounds in lords."—*Young.*

§ "Ce monde est un grand Bal, où des Fous déguisés,
Sous des risibles noms d'éminence, et d'altesse,
Pensent enfler leur etre et hausser leur bassesse."—*Voltaire.*

"Hast thou, O Sun, beheld an emptier sort,
Than such as swell this bladder of a court;
Such painted puppets, such a varnished race,
Of hollow gewgaws, only dress and face!"—*Donne.*

Such things that glitter like gilt gingerbread,
Should be with pap,* or else with kava fed.†
'Tis strange that those who manage court affairs,
Should not provide them clouts and cacking chairs.

Yes, this parade forms all the courtier's joys:
This royal baby-house of dress'd up toys.‡
Lord Fartlebury; Duke of Puddledock;
Prince Cacafogo; Countess Dillicock;
Lord Nincompoop; Sir George Golumpus Grub;
Veldt Marshal Hoggsgutz; Lady Trullibub;
Count Snickasnee; Lord Fudge; Prince Potowouskin;
Baron Bumfodder; Monsieur Mouschkin Poushkin;§
Lord Blath'rumskate; Earl Swipes; Count Doodledoo;
Madame Caca-du-Dauphin Baisemoncul;‖
The Rev'rend Noodle Doodle Dunderhead;
The Honorable Simon S . . . abed;
And Co.; for of them there's a numerous pack;
But these may serve as samples of the sack.

Lo! grandeur gives a feast: Oh, all ye gods,
Who peep down now and then from your abodes;

* "O folly, worthy of the nurse's lap,
Give it the breast, or cram its mouth with pap."—*Cowper.*

† Kava is a liquor in high estimation in the South Sea Islands, and is almost the exclusive beverage of the kings and royal tribes. It is made from the root of the pepper-tree; which, after being chewed by the natives, and the juice spit into a large bowl, is diluted with water."—See *Cook's Voyages.*

‡ "Round let us bound, for this is Punch's holiday,
Glory to Tom-foolery—huzza, huzza!"—*Rejected Addresses.*

It is hardly possible to caricature this childish stuff, or give an *outre* description of such full-grown babyism. Swift speaks of a *tiddidol* assemblage, where he was introduced. The queen (Brandy Nan), he says, stood in the middle of the circle, simpering and biting the edge of her fan; and looking, like an idiot, by turns at the drest-up dolls, who were standing all round the room like so many images.

§ The name of the Russian ambassador thirty or forty years ago.

‖ The dresses worn by all the ladies of *rank* and *fashion* some years ago, in that sink of vice and folly, Paris, were actually of this *delicate* color, at least as near as the dyers could match it—out of respect to the *royal* excrement.

Say, had ye ever up stairs in the sky,
Aught in the guttling way with this to vie ?*
Tho' at your sumptuous banquets with your goddesses,
Ye sat so cosy, without breech or boddices ;†
When were ye at your gormandizings able
To sport a river on your dining-table ?
Where, all amongst the gold and silver dishes,
Shoals could be seen of gold and silver fishes !
And all alive O !—not like fish-fag's sprats,
Fit only to be given to the cats. m
Yes, all alive ! though childish it may seem,
And *bona fide* swimming in the stream :
While noble lords and ladies, in amaze,
Upon the river and the fishes gaze.
" What taste !" cries Lord Fopdoodle ; " c'est unique !"

* At Carlton House, some years ago.

† The celestials were certainly very deficient in this respect, as many of them were nearly in *querpo* at their grand assemblies, where the Hebes and Ganymedes handed the nectar about. When breeches came first in use, is not exactly known. Moses was permitted to see the *back* parts of the great I AM; but we are not informed whether breeched or not. Adam is said to have worn green breeches; but that is meant merely as a witticism. Neither can we suppose Mister Noah wore inexpressibles, as in that *case* there would have been nothing for his son to have laughed at. The "man after God's own heart" was evidently bare about the dock, when he kicked up his heels and capered before the ark; since his wife ragged him for exposing his tackle to the maidens, and for which he said they would honor him.* That prophets were also of the *sans culotte* order is notorious; since Isaiah, one of the most celebrated, tramped about three years with his buttocks bare: not to mention many other instances in the holy Jew book. Homer speaks of breeches where Dr. Macshane attends the poor cuckold who is wounded in the posteriors by an arrow: since he tells us,

"The arrow's head, and greasy leather
Breeches, both came off together."—*Iliad*, book 4.

But whether the word *gubmuh*, in the original means breeches or not, is disputed; the learned disciples of the profound doctors, Parr and Porson, differing in opinion: some asserting the true meaning to be f—ting crackers; others insist on a—e-case being the genuine translation; while a third class of deep etymologists are equally positive that galligaskins is the true signification of the Greek word.

"Who shall decide when doctors disagree?"

And thus must this important matter be left.—*Ignoramus*.

* And of the maid-servants which thou hast spoken of: of them shall I be had in honor.—2 Sam. vi.

"Par Dieu!" exclaims Lord Froth, "c'est magnifique!"
"C'est bien joli!" sputters out another,
And one tom-fool still echoes to his brother.
The ladies too, while munching up their dinners,
Ask if the fish are pricklebacks, or minnows?
For those who were not near the river's brim,
Could not see how the little fishes swim,*
And frisk, "and vaggle all their pretty tails:"†
Not to please "baby Charles," but booby Wales!
Oh, grand celestials! Jupiter and Co.,
Say, had ye ever such a raree-show?

The "Lord's anointed" used, in times of old,
To keep a fool to laugh at, as we're told;
But now so many fools of lords are made,‡
Tom isn't wanted—they have spoiled his trade.
Provided with so choice a tom-fool train,
To keep an extra fool would be in vain;
With titled fools 'twould be mere waste of money—
Tom-fool at court's like sugar-sauce to honey.
Yet Tom's the most diverting; courtly fools
Are dress'd up dolls, who speak and move by rules;
Drill'd, strutting things, who scorn all mirth and jokes,
And never sport a grin like vulgar folks:
Laughter their buckram grandeur would destroy;
That way the "mob express their silly joy."§

* From the very crowded assemblage it may be supposed many of the ladies of quality were too distant from the margin of the river to peep in and ascertain the quality of the water animals.

† "Teazing made easy."

‡ "*Nature* exclaim'd with wonder—'*Lords* are things,
Which, never made by me, were made by kings.'"
Churchill.

§ "Loud laughter," says Chesterfield, "is extremely inconsistent with good manners: it is only the illiberal and noisy testimony of the joy of the *mob* at some very silly thing." And to the same tune singeth Lord Froth: "There is nothing," says this *noble* lord, "more unbecoming a man of *quality* than to laugh: it is such a vulgar expression of the passion! Everybody can laugh."—See the *Double Dealer*.

Even Bob, the doctor, since his apostacy, has affected the consequence of these high-born prigs, and joined the smirking coxcomb

Grand fools are stuff'd with "*manieres* and graces,"
Which surely make amends for vacant faces.

Of all the stupid follies brought from France,
The most disgusting is the "minuet" dance.
The poor automaton, with silly face,
Sprawls round its arms and legs, and calls it *grace!*
Now here, now there, affectedly it swings,
And seems a toyman's doll, on wheels and springs.
A glorious feat to swell the YAHOO's pride,
By which he's so completely monkeyfied!*

Oh, Chesterfield, thou most illustrious scribe!
First fiddle of the *a-la-puppy* tribe!
The world must surely deem it a disaster,
That thou wert not brought up a dancing-master;
The prince of capering coxcombs, great Marcel,†
Could not have taught the "graces" half so well;
Altho', like thee, he studied *bienséance*,
And was a true-bred Fribble, born in France.
How hast thou wrote, and wrote again, about it,
Tho' a respected Hottentot did flout it.‡
With trash like this didst thou take wondrous pains,
To cram thy son's skull with, instead of brains.
How didst thou scribble letter after letter,
But never found poor Phil§ a jot the better:
For—oh, ye gods, 'tis shocking to relate,
When at a dinner-party, in grand state,
He ate his cherry pie, then licked his plate!‖

tribe in their contempt of every thing *vulgar*. "Laughter," he exclaims, "is a *plebeian* emotion; nothing beyond a silent and transitory *simper* should be indulged in by the *refined* ranks!"—*Omniana.* One should suppose the laureat was *ironing* us, as Mrs. Slipslop terms it.

* Alfieri said he never could be taught by a French dancing-master, whose art once made him shudder and laugh. "If we reflect," says Mr. D'Israeli, "that, as it is now practised, it seems the art of giving affectation to a puppet, and that this puppet is a man, we can enter into this mixed sensation of degradation and ridicule."

† A celebrated dancing-master at Paris.

‡ Lord Chesterfield's appellation of the *great* moralist.

§ Philip Stanhope.

‖ Said to be a fact.

Such are "God's images" among the great;
The "lords of reason," puff'd with wealth and state.
But take your specimens from Mutton-lane,
Or Rotten-row,* and then be proud and vain.
Search Billingsgate, Saint Giles's, and Rag Fair,
And say what angel-forms you meet with there;
View them in dens where poverty prevails,
Or perishing in hospitals and jails;
See the poor cinder-sifter's filthy rags,
And chimney-sweepers, with their sooty bags;
A prey to squalid want, disease, and vermin,
(And thousands there are such for one in ermine).
Do these poor wretches, who eat husks like swine,
Display the boasted "human face divine?"†
Are "godlike heroes" found in their abodes?
O no! 'tis wealth makes YAHOOS demi-gods;
Of *godlike* qualities the poet sings,
But then they appertain to lords and kings.
Oh, what a blest, soul-gifted, sky-born race,
Sweeps in "God's image," and in Mudlark's grace!
In scavengers you "lords of reason" meet;
Vociferating "dust-ho" through the street!
"Creation's lords" divinely play their part,
And lift the fragrant bucket to the cart;
In spite of filth, *immortal souls* you trace,
Which glitter through the dirty shirt and face;
And though they stink, and have Tom ——dmen's looks,
They'll in the next world all be lords and dukes.‡

Inflated YAHOO! boast your blessed state,
Millions in rags and dirt—a few styled great;§

* Dens of misery in the vicinity of Clerkenwell, which, with Chick-lane and Black-boy Alley, will be in all probability swept away by the proposed new street from Fleet Market to Islington.

† Paradise Lost.

‡ "Blessed are the poor in spirit, for theirs is the kingdom of heaven."—Matt. v. 3.

§ Lord Byron has observed, that the world (speaking of England) seems only made for a few thousands called *quality*, or *rank* and *fashion*, as the West-enders are denominated.

But still they've so much feeling for each other,
My Lord Duke owns the Sweep his *Christian*-brother:
And though the poor are fed with fee-faw-fum,
They'll get a greasy chin in "kingdom-come."

Who would not give five pounds to treat a lord?
Though for a single peach, 'tis not absurd:
But give five shillings to the poor for bread,
Oh! that's disgraceful—up stairs *they'll* be fed,
And here perhaps it may not be amiss,
To add a fable in parenthesis;
A proverb even, if it comes in pat,
As Sancho tells the Don, is *verbum sat.*

A fox once met an ape, as Æsop says,
And chatter'd as they used in former days;
When, after compliments, the ape thus cried—
"I wish, kind sir, you'd peep at my backside:
You'll own I've little reason to be glad,
Considering my rump's so poorly clad.
I haven't got a tail that's worth a rush,
While you've a superfluity of brush;
And could you but a little morsel spare,
To cover my poor buttocks, now so bare,
I certainly should take it very kind,
As then I should be *comme il faut* behind."
"God zounds!" quoth Reynard, flying in a passion,
"An ape, forsooth! and would be dress'd fox-fashion!
A very pretty joke for plebs like thee
To dizen out, and think to rival me!
No, no, my brush may trail along the ground,
But not an atom of it shall be found
To decorate the riff-raff, my inferiors;
Much more to hide a stinking ape's posteriors."

This fable to the YAHOO may apply,
As any one will see with half an eye;
"Id est," if he has "quantum suff." of brain:
And now we'll to our *moutons** turn again.

* Rabelais.

Folly and vice by turns the YAHOO rule,
Sometimes the knave prevails, sometimes the fool.
Actions that often are considered good,
Base would be found, the motives understood:*
His life's a counterfeit, a masquerade,†
And cant and rank hypocrisy a trade.
With artificial phiz he acts a part,
And all through life his tongue belies his heart:‡
"Volto sciolto," says my lord to Phil,§
"Ma pensieri stretti," mind that still.
His character completely would you know,
Read Swift, and Mandeville, and Rochefoucault.‖
Observe yon black-dress'd Yahoos, what grimace!
Mirth in the heart, and sorrow in the face
What signs of woe, crape hat-bands, solemn walk,
Exteriors dismal—hearts as light as cork.¶

* "All the virtues that have ever been in mankind," says Swift, 'may be counted upon a few fingers; but their follies and vices are innumerable, and time adds hourly to the heap." And what says brother parson of the present day? "The world and almost everything in it are capable of being abused by *man*, whose corrupt propensities are continually leading him to poison the sources of his own happiness."—*Sumner.*

† "Our life is a false nature—'tis not in
The harmony of things."—*Byron.*

‡ Nous aurions souvent honte de nos plus belles actions, si le monde voyait tous les motifs qui les produisent."—*Rochefoucalt.*

§ See "Lord Chesterfield's Letters to his Son," to qualify him for the *beau-monde.*

‖ The proceedings of the good, honest church-going YAHOOS toward each other, are truly described by Mandeville in the story of the two sugar merchants, letter B in the Fable of the Bees, verifying the Italian proverb,

"Con Arte ed Inganni si vive il mezzo anni;
Con Inganni e con Arte si vive l'altre parti."

"What think you," says Horace Walpole, "of the cruelty and villany of European settlers; but this very morning I found that part of the purchase of Maryland from the *savage* proprietors (for *we* do not massacre, *we* are such good Christians as only to cheat), was a quantity of red lead and a parcel of jews'-harps."—*Walpole's Correspondence.*

"Ovunque il guardo osservato tu giri,
Scorticatori e scorticati miri:
Gl'imbelli il forte, ed i babbei lo scaltro,
E insomma ognun che può, scortica l'altro."—*Casti.*

¶ "Heredis fletus sub personâ risus est."

A gouty friend (oh, what delightful luck),
Has left the world, and left him all his muck.
Heart-broken they *must seem*, and in a tone
Of whining, tell you of their *dear friend* gone.
In sables then they're deck'd from top to toe,
That every one their great distress may know:
And while in canting strain they seem to grieve,
(What mockery) they're laughing in their sleeve.*

But the grand farce is when a monarch dies—
A butch'ring Harry, or a George the wise;
A royal Tiger, or a royal Neddy;
No matter which, the scutcheons are got ready;
The carcass lays in state, with mutes and lights;
For loyal subjects love such pretty sights.
Crushing each other's ribs in crowds they go,
Though full of grief they long to see the show.
And when the royal carrion's in the tomb,
The undertaker's garb they all assume;
The grov'ling crew throughout the royal nation,
Show outward signs of inward lamentation.
At church, at play-house, and at public shows,
The "lords of reason" all as black as crows,
Look as if Nick had shook his soot-bag o'er 'em,
To make them like himself—for *black's decorum*.
Hence Latitats and Parsons when they clack,
Out of respect to Nick, are dress'd in black;
For though these long-robed gentry all pretend
To hate Old Blackey, he's their dearest friend.
(Were YAHOOS free from vice they would not want
The lawyer's jargon, or the parson's cant).†

* "In all civil societies men are taught insensibly to be hypocrites from their cradle. Nobody dares to own that he gets by public calamities, or even by the loss of private persons. The sexton would be stoned should he wish openly for the death of the parishioners, though everybody knew he had nothing else to live upon."—*Search into Society*, 402. May not the same be said of doctors and physicians, who profess to be very *glad* when they meet their friends and acquaintance in good health?

† "Why were laws made, but that we are rogues by nature."—*Shakspere.*

After all the blarney of the *immortal* bard about the Yahoo's perfec-

'Tis true, they call him dragon, serpent, shark;
But then they shake hands with him in the dark.

Now Old Nick's *black* in grain, a knowing prig,
Who hides his horns and tail with gown and wig;*
And meeting with young Chip† (the Lamb) one day,
He whipt him on his back, and flew away:
Then in a wilderness for forty days,‡
He tried to *diddle* him in various ways;
With promised kingdoms, if he would adore him,
And *boo* respectfully, and fall before him;
But Chippy, though a Lamb, was not a flat,
For through the gown and wig he smelt a rat,
So neither made a leg, nor doff'd his hat;
But cried, "I smell your brimstone, Master Nick;
You're after playing me some shabby trick:
Don't think with your palaver you can blind me,
But hold your jaw, my cock, and get behind me."§

Ben Johnson says, that Beelzebub an ass is,‖
Though for a conjurer with fools he passes;
And sure he proved himself a Johnny Raw,
To let young Chippy thus slip through his paw:

tions, who would have thought he would have let the cat out of the bag, and like the Satyr in the fable, "blow hot and cold with the same mouth."

* "To hinder him from being known,
He borrowed parson Squintum's gown;
These kind of robes, his godship knew,
Hide rogues the best, and roguery too."
Homer Burlesqued.

† The carpenter's son.

‡ "Then was Jesus led up of the Spirit into the wilderness to be tempted of the devil; and when he had fasted forty days and forty nights, he was afterward an hungered. Again the devil taketh him up into an exceeding high mountain, and showeth him all the kingdoms of the world and the glory of them: and saith unto him, All these things will I give thee, if thou wilt fall down and worship me." —Matt. iv.

§ "And Jesus answered and said unto him, Get thee behind me, Satan."—Luke iv.

‖ Comedy of "The Devil's an Ass."

And after, when, as Christian creeds all tell,
He had him three days in his claws in hell;
Yet, like a blockhead, let him scamper out,
When he a treaty might have made no doubt.
With such a first-rate prisoner in limbo,
He might have strutted with his arms a-kimbo:
Not only haggled for his liberation,
But have released his staff for their damnation!
Yet who can judge for this proud cock? they say,
That every one has some odd whim or way.
"De gustibus non disputandum est,"
He might think his warm corner much the best;
Where he could smoke his pipe, and swill his toddy,
Nor longer care a fig for any body.
He had had trumpeting enough before,
Blasting and puffing till his throat was sore;
And now preferr'd, bored with their "holy, holy,"
The Bumble-puppy game, and Rolly-polly.
But this is all digressive—we'll go back
To where we talk'd of Yahoos wearing black.
Young Chip it seems smelt Nick, and didn't mind him,
But snubb'd him well, and bid him get behind him.
While to commemorate this dire event,
Christians wear charcoal-colored clothes in Lent:
Nor dare they then taste any luscious dish,
But snuffle grace o'er parsnips and salt fish;
While on Black Friday, by saints nick-nam'd *Good*,
Buns, gallows-marked, are deemed soul-saving food:*
Till penance over, Easter brings delight,
And then they gorge and guzzle day and night.

Thus six months past (the grieving time requir'd
For kings), the Yahoos of their black get tir'd;
The mockery no longer is display'd—
They then find out that "*it makes* bad for trade,"

* Notwithstanding the *spread*, and the *stream*, and *march of intellect*, and the so much boasted enlightened age, there is scarcely a family in England in which this superstitious and degrading mummery is omitted on what is called Good Friday, when the streets resound with the cries of *Hot Cross Buns!* But hogs delight in garbage.

Besides, although he was the "best of kings,"
They're not to fret their guts to fiddle-strings.
So grief adieu—a royal chamberlain
Says, "NEDDY's put your gaudy's on again."
Th' obsequious herd, impatient of delay,
Resume their fripp'ry, and as larks are gay,
Proud to show off in this lickspittle farce,
And mourn a Nero, or a royal ass.
In black, or colors, still they're strutting seen,
Puff'd with conceit, and proud of being mean.
For, though it seems a paradox, 'tis true,
The self-same Yahoo's mean and haughty too;
With vices opposite, he's doubly curst,
"Meanness that soars, and pride that licks the dust."

Observe that buckram'd, whisker-jawed, queer thing,
He's called a "lord in waiting" to the king;
And when his majesty's dispos'd to stir,
This thing sticks to his crupper like a bur:
Whether the monarch marches fast or slow,
Just the same pace this lackey-lord must go;
And at the play-house, when the king goes there,
Skip-kennel stands upright behind his chair:
Scarce daring, while he stands in stiff-rump'd state,
To turn from side to side his empty pate:
Abject, yet proud, a mixty-maxty thing;
But very fit to wait upon a king.
Among the court-gang crawling like a toad,
A three-tailed bashaw in his own abode:
An abject reptile in the drawing-room;
At home the tyrant's manner he'll assume:
A very Bobadil, a Bully-back;
But when at court, he sails on t'other tack:
Booing and cringing, none so mild and meek,
Not brother Bruin then, but Jerry Sneak.

God made man in his image, parsons teach,
When Old Nick came next day and kick'd his breech;
And, being "maitre Charlatan," alas!
Soon got *God's image* bundled out to grass.

For he was in a garden placed at first,
'Till by the snake's contrivance he was curs'd.
(The *quomodo* has been before related,
Where madame Eve was found to be soft-pated).
And claiming still the Yahoo as his prize,
This devil-snake we now apostrophize.

O, thou infernal omnipresent dragon !*
A mighty feat it is for thee to brag on,
To gull a naked nincompoopish couple,
By coaxing them to eat a bit of apple.
Thou sooty, smutty, worst of bugaboos,
Who's at the Yahoo's heels where'er he goes ;
Whether call'd Old One, Nick, or Scratch, or Devil,
'Tis thou that dost incline his heart to evil.
Not only hast thou dosed him well with pride,
But most of thy *good* qualities beside.
Had it not been for thee, thou ugly toad,
This world of ours had been a snug abode ;
But since thou trottest night and day about,
In ev'ry corner poking thy damn'd snout,
The Yahoo's never safe, but ev'ry minute
Finds something wrong, and cries "the devil's in it."
The Lord, we're told, once cramm'd thee in thy den,
Then, who the devil let thee out again ?†
But 'tis no use for us to growl and grumble,
If fated, in thy clutches we must tumble.
Does not the saint of saints, the frenzied Paul,‡

* Would not the omnipresence of the black monarch, since he is universally acknowledged as a Ubiquitarian, be an excellent subject for the pen of an evangelical fustian scribbler?

† "To credit such idle whims," says the Indian, "is an affront to the great Spirit, as it charges him with authorizing mischief, by being the direct author of all the disorders and wickednesses in the world, by suffering the evil spirit to get out of hell."—*Lahonton's Voyage.*

‡ "How little did those people think, who saw
The first appearance of this crooked lout;
Who saw this same disturber of the law,
When first from town to town he rov'd about.

Insinuate that we're predestinated all,*
From birth, the chosen few aloft to go,
The many sous'd into the pit below?†
The *sheep* elected, all cram'd up to heaven;
The *goats* rejected, down to hell are driv'n.‡
But let us leave this jargon to the schools:
To rev'rend prigs who dub each other fools.
They'll solve such mysteries beyond a doubt,
And where there is no meaning, find one out;
Prove that it's dark at noon, and light at night.
And tho' all's wrong, "whatever is, is right."
Prate about "trees of life," and "trees of knowledge,"
(Else wherefore go such loggerheads to college),§
What Paul saw when he up to heaven was skipping;
And why he *mags* so much on *doodle*-snipping.‖

Ah, little did they think how deep the root,
How far 'twas doom'd to spread, how curs'd the fruit.
* * * * * *
"Yet so it is; a Paul has liv'd and died;
A curs'd religion has sprung up and rent
The world with factions—men have fought and pray'd
As with one breath: their energies they've spent
In brutalizing wars, where hellish strife
Could prompt each man to seek a brother's life."
Prize Poem on the Life and Character of St. Paul.

* Moreover, whom he did predestinate,—them he also called.—Romans viii.

Therefore hath he mercy on whom he will have mercy; and whom he will, he hardeneth.—Romans ix.

Israel hath not obtained that which he seeketh for, but the *election* hath obtained it. God hath given them the spirit of slumber, eyes that they should not see, and ears that they should not hear, unto this day.—Romans xi.

† Straight is the gate, and narrow is the way that leadeth unto life, and few there be that find it.

‡ And he shall set the sheep on his right hand, but the goats on the left. Then shall he say unto them on his left hand, Depart from me ye cursed into everlasting fire, prepared for the devil and his angels. —Matt. xxv.

§ "Else wherefore breathe I in a Christian land?"—*Richard III.*

‖ A great part of the frothy epistles; or, as Cardinal Bembo very properly called them, Epistolacciæ of this holy maniac, are filled with disgusting balderdash respecting the profitableness of circumcision; which, indeed, as the godly cock was a bit of a snipper himself, having

Of Old Nick's *somerset*, and sin original
(The leading trumps with which the parsons *pigeon all*):
How to "cast off the old man," they'll explain;
And solve the slang of "being born again"—
Of faith, foreknowledge, grace, and free-will bawl,
Till it's as clear as mustard to us all.

Whether the Yahoo's folly, or his pride,
Most governs, 'tis not easy to decide;
But in the high-born race, 'tis plainly shown,
Excess of pride* stamps *them* the devil's own;
Pride governs *these* through life, and strange to tell,
Outweighs the terrors both of death and hell!

Two *noble* lords, sworn friends, sit down to play,
(Both good church-going Christians in their way).
But if, as oft it happens, words arise,
And one affirms what t'other lord denies;
Then anger's kindled, hateful passion grows,
And Christian friends are chang'd to bitter foes.
Urged by false honor, let who will be right,
The challeng'd has no option but to fight;‡

operated upon poor Tim, by depriving him of his foreskin (Acts xvi.), is not so much to be wondered at. But why did not the saint explain this holy business to his beloved sisters in the Lord, Priscilla, Mary, and the rest of the chosen vessels, whom he desires may be saluted with a holy kiss.—Romans xvi.

* "There is no danger so great, but by the help of his pride a man may slight and confront it; nor any manner of death so terrible, but with the same assistance he may court, and if he has a firm constitution undergo, it with alacrity."—*Fable of the Bees.*

"La plus calamiteuse et fragile de toutes les créatures," says Montaign, "c'est l'homme, et quant la plus orgueilleuse.—Il me semble à la vérité, que Nature, pour la consolation de notre estat des miserable et chetif, ne nous ait donné en partage que la présumption."—*Essais*, liv. 2, chap. 12.

† "How comes it that a man of honor should so readily accept of a challenge, when in the prime of life and in perfect health? It is his pride that conquers his fear: for when his pride is not concerned, this fear will appear most glaringly. If he is not used to the sea, let him but be in a storm; or, if he never was ill before, have but a slight fever, and he'll show a thousand anxieties, and in them the inestimable value he sets on life."—*Search into Society*, 383.

"Un homme religieux n'est-il pas bien sûr de sa damnation éter-

And some so skilfully the weapons handle,
At twenty paces they can snuff a candle.
So trained to murder in a genteel way,
You may have *satisfaction* any day;
Giving the injured party who complains,
Redress, by coolly blowing out his brains.
Now where's their *Christian* love? does worldly pride
Set *holy gospel* precepts all aside?
While thus to blind revenge, and murder giv'n,
Are they e'er checked by thoughts of hell or heaven?
Do these "Corinthians" in such affairs,
Before they shoot each other, say their pray'rs?
Oh, no! they laugh at all the parson's stuff—
They're *high-born* Yahoos, and quite "up to snuff."*

Yes, vice and folly tinge the heart and brain,
And leave behind an everlasting stain.
Adam, we're told, sought wisdom, and was blam'd;†
He ate the apple, and his race was damn'd;‡
If he was not permitted to be wise,
Surely his offspring wisdom may despise.

nelle s'il est tué en duel? Et cependant l'honneur l'importe, et il se bat!"—*M. de Rivarol.*

* As such high-born prigs are always (as well as the low-born) well stuffed with gospel mammon at their schools and colleges, how comes it they can so easily shake it all off, and send one another to hell so deliberately? They should at least take a parson with them upon such occasions, to intercede with the Lamb in behalf of their precious souls, which are thus precipitated into the fiery lake in *sæcula sæculorum.*

† "Lesoing de s'augumenter en sagesse et en science, ce fut la première ruine du genre humain: c'est la voye par où il s'est précipité à la damnation eternelle."—*Montaigne.*

‡ Of all the absurdities that ever were foisted upon the imagination of a Yahoo, this apple story is the most completely ridiculous? Adam should undoubtedly have been taught to seek knowledge, nor shun it, that thereby he might have avoided evil. If his instructor had been an evil genius, the interdiction would have been in character, as ignorance is the parent of crime and misery. "Quand on fait reflection," says Voltaire, "que presque toute la terre a été infatuée de pariels contes, et qu'ils ont fait l'education du genre humain, on trouve les fables de Pilpay et d'Esope bien rasonnables."

We ought, 'tis plain, from such good scripture rules,
To bring up all our children arrant fools.*
And this has been the case since Adam's time;
To doubt, or speak the truth, is deem'd a crime.
'Tis true, we've scores of metaphysic fools,
From Brazen-nose and Corpus-Christi schools:†
All filled with learned ignorance and pride,‡
A. B.'s, L. D.'s, and Lord knows what beside;
Who with big wigs their owlish phizzes cook so,
That if they are not wise, they try to look so.§
They jabber about *faith*, by which is meant
That you should give them credit for their cant;
For faith's not worth a fig which can't dispense,
With things that give the lie to common sense.
'Tis against reason, is it? that's enough;
A parson's creed demands no better proof.
Faith's the grand nostrum for the parson's jobs,
And moves all "stumbling-blocks" from Yahoos' nobs.
Well stuff'd with faith, and larded with devotion
You in a walnut-shell may cross the ocean:
If ye doubt not, cry *geehup* when you will,
And Highgate hops to Harrow on the Hill.‖

* "For in much wisdom is much grief; and he that increaseth knowledge increaseth sorrow."—Eccles. i. 18.

† Brazen-faced would have been a more suitable appellation. What names for colleges of instruction! *Body of Christ!* This wretched kind of superstitious mummery is carried to such an extent in the Catholic countries, that their inns and fighting ships are sanctified with the precious epithets of "Blood of Christ," "Holy Ghost," and "Savior of the World," &c.

‡ "It may sound oddly," says Lord Bolingbroke, "but it is true in many cases to say, that if men had learned less their way to knowledge would be shorter and easier. There is no cure for one who is taught to be a blockhead; his ignorance is the fruit of instruction; he has clogged his mind with learned darkness, and verifies the proverb, that *merus scholaticus est merus asinus.*—See *Independent Whig,* vol. i. pp. 2 and 258.

§ "Thus pedants will hang out a solemn face,
To put off nonsense with a better grace."—*Young.*

‖ "Jesus said, If ye have faith and doubt not, ye shall say unto this mountain, Be thou removed, and be thou cast into the sea, and it shall be done."—See *Questions,* viii. 119.—Mark xi.

The little hills by Faith will skip like lambs,
And all the mountains dance like rams ;*
To those with Faith all contradiction bends,†
A walking-stick may be without two ends.
Charcoal milk-white, and snow as black as jet;
A brewer's horse may in a bottle get;
A man may jump down his own throat, and then
(If it so please the Lord) jump up again.
Faith at impossibilities ne'er wrangles,
But sees distinctly round and square triangles!
Faith's the FA TUTTO, priestcraft's corner-stone;
Take that away, and presto! all is gone.
Call it credulity, the tribe roar out,
All in full chorus, "*They* are damn'd who doubt."
That doubt is nothing but the devil's snare,
And skeptics all in hell, with old Voltaire;

* "Why hop ye so, ye high hills?"—Psalm lxviii. "The mountains skipped like rams, and the little hills like lambs."—Psalm lxviii. This silly bombast is called sublime; so that there does not seem a straw to choose between nonsense and sublimity. Homer abounds in trash of this sort (one of the reasons why he is so much admired); where not only horses are weeping and discoursing, but even rivers get up and come to the "scratch," one (Xanthus) calling the other (Simois) to his assistance. Nonsense seems to amalgamate with the putty-like stuff in the skulls of the lords of reason, who are sure to delight in any thing in proportion to its absurdity; their precious faith enabling them by obumbrating and offuscating (as Pomposo phrases it) their intellects, to see apple-dumplings when there is only horse dung before their snouts! Wonderful Yahoo! thy gullibility exceeds all power of imagination.

† "La vertu fondementale de toute religion, *i. e.*, la plus utile à ses ministres c'est la FOI. Elle consiste dans une credulité sans bornes, qui fait croire sans examen tout ce que les interprêtes de la divinité out interet que l'on croie. La FOI impliçite a été la source des plus grands attentats qui se soient commis sur la terre."—*Le Bon Sens.*

"Credulity, call'd faith, entraps the soul;
She lies in wait for idiotism and youth;
List'neth to tales baptized rigmarole,
And makes them pass for oracles of truth."—*Pindar.*

"Doubt," says Bolingbroke, "is the key of knowledge: who do not doubt will never examine; and those who never examine will never know, but remain in perpetual ignorance.—*Philosophical Essays.*

Lament there's not a HOLY inquisition,
To burn blasphemers in this wicked nation.*

Such are our teachers, rev'rend sapient prigs;
Starch'd, formal things, in loop'd hats, bands, and wigs:
Such are the Mentors of our public schools;
Is it a wonder Yahoos are such fools?
They'll tell you it was from pride that Satan fell,
And that the rich with Dives are in hell.
Style themselves plenipos from great Jehovah,
And while they face their dupes, all live in clover.†

Surrounded by this moon-eyed gaping rabble,
Who prick their asses' ears up at his gabble,
See Rowland Hill squint upward to the sky,
Like Macbeth at his dagger, and then cry,
"Dearly beloved, mark well what I say,
Cast off the *old man;* ye must fast and pray:

* "But saints now persecute—those who won't turn
To their idolatry, they hang and burn.
They were not so at first—they could not be:
They wanted power: this obtained, we find
Their character appear'd: from fear once free,
The damning curse began, which sunk mankind
Beneath—aye, speak! to hide this truth were vain—
Beneath the lowest brute that stalks the plain.
Call'd civilized! far better had ye been
Like beasts that perish; then ye would have liv'd
And rov'd in harmony through wood and glen;
Nor would ye for the future then have griev'd:
Or had ye fought it would have been for food,
And not for creeds ye never understood."—*Prize Poem.*

† We need not wonder at the audacity of this tribe of black locusts, when we consider that "kings and queens" are to be their "nursing fathers and mothers, and are to bow their faces to the earth, and lick the dust off their feet." No wonder the Holy Bible is so industriously crammed into the maws of the besotted Yahoos, and so much holy zeal displayed in converting the heathen! But if kings and queens are to "lick the dust off their feet," how are the swinish multitude to show *their* respect to the Lord's ambassadors? Why, by licking *somewhere* else to be sure. Il n'y a pas d'autre moyen; and so they ought, in order to keep them in proper subjection.—Laud exhibited himself in his true colors when in the height of his career, he insolently said, he hoped to see the time when the greatest jack-gentleman in the land should not dare to stand with his hat on before the meanest priest.

Ye're born in sin, and very prone to evil,
And but for me, ye'd soon be with the devil;
But heed him not, for all his rant and racket,
The Lord's appointed me to dust his jacket.
Bring but your filthy lucre to the church,
And we'll soon leave the rascal in the lurch:
Renounce the world, and all its empty trash;
Good pious Christians never can want cash!
The Scripture moveth us in sundry places,
To give the parson ALL without wry faces:*
The holy gospel proves it's not a fib,
'Twas so with Ananias and his rib;
They wanted for themselves to keep a penny,
Tho Holy Ghost said 'No! ye sha'n't have any.'
So down they tumbled like two cheating wretches,
(Those who defraud the church the devil fetches).
Don't think I tip ye holy gospel gammon,
In order to cajole ye of your mammon:
I scorn to meddle with your worldly pelf,
I never want a farthing for myself.
Poor souls, indeed, in this world I know many,
Who smell meat in cook's shops, but ne'er taste any.

* "Godliness is great gain." "Bring me all thou hast and follow me is the true church maxim," says Gordon. "As many as were possessed of houses or lands sold them, and brought the prices of the things that were sold, and laid them down at the apostles' feet!"

This is in the true spirit of holy religion! Bring ALL, you can not bring too much, as was barefacedly avowed by John Wesley. "You," says the pious holder-forth, "who have £200 a year, and spend but one, do you give God the other hundred? If not, you rob him of just so much. Oh, leave nothing behind you! Send all you have before you go into a better world! Lend it! lend it ALL unto the Lord, and it shall be paid you again. Haste, haste, my beloved; haste, lest you should be called away before you have settled what you have on this security. When this is done, you may boldly say, Now I have nothing to do but to die! [True enough, John.] Father, into thy hands I commit my spirit! come, Lord Jesus, come quickly."—*Southey's Life of Wesley.*

We may well say with Cowper—

"Legates and delegates with pow'rs from hell,
Tho' heavenly in pretension, fleece us well."

Or with Doddsley—

"The holy drones monopolize the sky,
And plunder by a vow of poverty."

Do, my beloved, pity their hard fate,
And drop for them your money in the plate.*
Remember you've your blessed Savior's word,
Give to the poor you lend unto the Lord."

Oh, pious preachers, reverendissimos,
Do give the rabble some religious shows,
And, pope-like, let them kiss your holy toes.
How very much ye all by your behavior,
Observe the precepts of your "blessed Savior."
What self-denial! modest, mild, and meek;
Ye never riches, or Commendams seek;
Ye never wish to swell your worldly store,
But give whate'er ye get to feed the poor;
And call in all the crippled and the blind,
Whene'er ye guttle, as ye are enjoin'd.†
Ye've no vile appetites to gratify;
Temptations of the devil ye defy.
All worldly vanities ye shun with care,
Brown-bread and gospel-sauce is precious fare;
Ye never stuff your guts at tavern dinners,
"Christ and a Crust" is quite enough for sinners;‡
Ye never swill, nor gormandize like beasts,
As greasy cits do, at their Lord May'r's feasts.
If ye have double chins, and swagging paunches,
It's not with calapash, nor luscious haunches;
Ye poke no spoon in any rich men's dishes,
Nor play the sycophant for loaves and fishes;

* "'Tis the saint's godly maxim to beg for the pelf,
In behalf of the poor, and then keep it himself."

† "When thou makest a dinner or a supper, call not thy friends, nor thy rich neighbors; call the maimed, the poor, the lame and the blind."—Luke xiv. Ay, catch'em at it! a pretty rig to see all the beggars in Lambeth sitting nose to nose with his grace of Canterbury, forsooth!

‡ Many of the mawworm tribe have these cant phrases in their mouths, and boast of the riches of "Christ and a Crust," which they possess, and which their fleecing parsons tell them is quite sufficient, and all a good Christian needs. Bedlam is half-filled with these poor creatures; and the number of *out* patients affected with the same *virus* (which Voltaire aptly denominates *la verole morale*) is incredible.

But mortify your flesh by pray'r and fasting,
In order to obtain life everlasting.

Such are our teachers and our preachers too!
All men of *gumption*—give the dev'l his due;*
With Bible, blunderbuss, and Pray'r-book sabre,
Poor Beelzebub's black hide they all belabor;
While he, who knows that this is humbug stuff,
Snaps his black fingers at their bounce and huff:
For that, however, they pretend to scout him,
They couldn't carry on their trade without him:
So to his valet Smut (who combs his wigs
And shaves him) says, "Go, tell the pulpit prigs
I value not their gospel-mag a louse,
But take their sermons to the little house;
To buffet me they only lose their pains,
And show they're better stuff'd with guts than brains;
But if they are for coming to the *Scratch*,
By God I'll curry the whole *blackguard* batch."†

Who, my lord bishop can with pride reproach,
Altho' he lives in state, and keeps his coach?
Does he not with a pious phiz declare,
That filthy lucre's nothing but a snare?

* "Men that can strut it and look big,
With store of guts as well as wig."—*Homer.*

† As these reverend devil-boxers are dressed in black, and are *guards* to the church, the Black Prince's epithet, if not very polite, is at least very appropriate.

"Sure 'tis an orthodox opinion,
That grace is founded in dominion.
Great piety consists in pride;
To *rule* is to be sanctified:
To domineer and to control
Both o'er the body and the soul,
Is the most perfect discipline
Of church rule, and by *right divine.*
For saints may do the same thing by
The spirit in sincerity,
Which other men are tempted to,
And at the devil's instance do;
And yet the actions be contrary,
Just as the saints and wicked vary."—*Hudibras.*

"Nolo episcoparii" is his boast;
But then he's called on by the Holy Ghost;*
And when a ghost calls with such special news,
How can a bishop in his heart refuse?
Renouncing vanities and sinful lust,
His treasure's where there's neither "moth nor rust;"
He scorns all mammon (just as dogs do mutton);
But seeks it with the stomach of a glutton.
He never makes provision for the morrow,
But gives away his all, the Lord to follow;
In mien so lowly, and so truly meek,
When struck on one he turns the other cheek;
Each angry and revengeful feeling smothers,
Nor e'er resents the trespasses of others.†
But watch this canting tribe, and if you've eyes,
You'll find all this mere fudge and humbug lies—
Mark well the conduct of these tithe-collectors,
From high to low, archbishops, deans, and rectors:
You'll soon perceive the glaring contradiction,
And that their ghostly jabber's all a fiction.

* What a stock of brass these reverends must be endowed with, to pronounce in the most solemn manner, and in the face of day, that they are unwilling to become bishops; when at the same time it is well known that they have been exerting themselves in every way possible to obtain the mitre. Shame, where is thy blush? Talk of the impudence of a highwayman's horse! bah; transfer the comparison to a parson.

† Only now and then, when the devil gets the ascendency over these Lord's embassadors, as happened lately *near* Twickenham, where the Rev. ——— prosecuted his gardener for stealing two-penny worth of beef, of which he was convicted; the parson having found the slice of meat in his possession, and carefully fitted it to the round from which it had been cut. But instances of clerical charity, forgiveness of trespasses, and compassionate feeling for the poor, abound. A *worthy* rector (of Blue-coat school notoriety), within one hundred miles of Edmonton, who has only about £2,000 per annum, threatened his gardener with legal punishment for making free with a few potatoes not long since! While another worthy of the sable corps, not far from Leatherhead, and who is moreover a *just-ass*, fined a poor laboring man nine shillings for selling a few cherries, which grew in his own garden, on the Lord's day. What a blessing the *Lord's* day is to the poor—in *spirit!* No wonder the swinish multitude are all so eager to salute the posteriors of their spiritual pastors, before they can even slip down their unmentionables.

Of such you'll always find the tongue and heart,
Like east and west, lie very far apart.*
And verifies what Hobbes said long ago,
That words would with a fool for money go:
But with the wise would not so easy pass,
They smelt the diff'rence soon 'twixt gold and brass.†

The YAHOO, as if prompted by the devil,
To physical has added moral evil;
His self-tormenting mind is on the stretch
To plague himself, and be his own Jack Ketch.
What he thinks wrong to-day, to-morrow's right;
He loves at noon what he detests at night:
The fiend that plagues him, his own sickly brain,
Turns all his schemes of pleasure into pain.
A slave to all the follies of the great,
Whate'er they do he's sure to imitate.
Tell him, 'mongst lords and dukes it is the mode,
He'll walk upon his head, or eat a toad.‡
Should any blockhead cut his coat in half,
When he walk'd out the rabble all would laugh,
But tell them 'tis a lord, the ape-like crew,
To look like him, cut all their coats in two.§
FASHION's the magic word; if some grand fool
Is all be-whisker'd, it becomes the rule:
The YAHOOS all then try to gain applause,
By looking like baboons about the jaws.‖

* "Is there a churchman who on God relies,
Whose life his faith and doctrine justifies?
Not one." *Lord Rochester.*

† It was an observation of Hobbes, that words "were the counters of wise men, and the money of fools."

‡ Doddsley's Poems.

§ It is said, Lord Spencer, for a wager, to prove the folly of the Yahoo, as to fashion, in imitating the *upper orders*, actually appeared in the public places in a half coat, *i. e.*, with the skirts cut off; and, in a very short time, everybody followed the example, and appeared in a similar dress; which was, from that circumstance, dubbed a Spencer.

‖ Whiskers are manufactured at present, and dyed to any color for such as may want them in haste, when they are stuck on! Vast improvements.

Ask one of these brute-snouted prigs, what news?
He'll tell you Hoby makes the smartest shoes:
Or should you want an exquisite cut coat,
Stultz is your man, when tipp'd a ten-pound note.
See dear Miss Tommy dressing!—what's he at?
Why, studying how to tie on his cravat:
Of modes there are no less than thirty-six,*
And Tommy doesn't know on which to fix!
What "march of mind!" what scientific days!
Women wear boots, and long-back'd lubbers stays.

Folly, thy name is *Yahoo*—thou dost show
Thyself conspicuous both in belle† and beau.
The females, with their form dissatisfied,
(And half-deranged through piety and pride,)
By pads, cork-rumps, and lacing-tight, pretend
The shape that nature gave them they can mend;
And who'll dispute the female Yahoo's taste,
Who barters health to gain a slender waist!
Screw'd in so tight they scarce can draw their breath,
Persisting, even though it threaten death.
All tops and bottoms, nothing now will do,
Unless, like wasps, they're nearly cut in two.
In shape an hour-glass, pinch'd up in the middle,
And puff'd out round the shoulders and bum-fiddle!
As if for Venus-Hottentots design'd,
They hang a full-stuffed pocket on behind.
Each to be foremost in the folly brags,
Huge bushel bonnets—sleeves like pudding-bags!
"Gigot de mouton" call'd, of Paris fame,
Though "jambe de bœuf" would be a fitter name.

* A book is advertised, called, the "Art of tying on a Cravat," price 3s., in which there are thirty-two modes exhibited on plates, with a "History of the Cravat from its Origin to the present Time," &c.; with a portrait of the author! which has run through three editions. Oh, intellect, no wonder there is so much boasting of thy spread.

† "Frailty, thy name is woman," says the *divine* bard; but why not man? The females do certainly crowd most into the Gospel-shops; many, no doubt, from the fear of the devil, and many from vanity to display their finery; but are the puppies of the masculine gender much behind them in absurdity?

If French, howe'er preposterous or frightful,
The Yahoo belles all cry, "Oh, how delightful!"

Observe those coxcombs all so slowly pacing,
To show off—'tis the funeral of a Mason.
With leather aprons, compasses, and rules,
By which to prove that they're no *common* fools;
With antics that would make the devil grin,
They're at an ale-house what is call'd "*tiled-in.*"
Building a temple then to *work* they go,
To imitate king Solomon's in show.
The great Jew king was pleas'd with apes we find,*
And these are their descendants left behind:
Some say they're with hot pokers mark'd—why not?
When we behold the Yahoo such a sot.†

Absorb'd in follies, but yet never stated,
The Yahoo's first with *this*, then *that* elated.
One childish fancy after t'other's tried,
Be-pictur'd now, and now be-butterfly'd;
Be-shell'd, be-fiddled, magnetizing next;
Seeking amusement still, and still perplex'd.

* "Every three years once came the ships of Tarshish bringing gold and silver, and apes, and peacocks."—2 Chron. ix.

If these wiseacres were to exhibit a model of the royal Jews' seraglio it would be highly amusing, with the apartments for his thousand belles!

"Where Solomon in wisdom shines,
Among his wives and concubines;
A thousand only? what a quantum
To play with him at rantum-skantum!
Sure wenches then were ten a-penny,
When this Jew king could get so many.
One should have guess'd, as gold was plenty,
He might have had eighteen or twenty,
But such a *posse!* zounds and blood!
Enough to drive him mad, by God.
Smouch might be rich, perhaps; but *wise!*
Oh, no! the ghost may tell us lies—
Peacocks and apes he might possess:
But sure of wisdom no man less."

† "Oh! we are ridiculous animals! and if angels have any fun in them, how we must divert them."—*Horace Walpole.*

Through F. S. A.'s old lumber then he blunders,
Like Katerfelto's cat,* announcing "wonders!"
Buys an old p— pot fashion'd "a la Grecque,"
From Herculaneum dug, a true antique!
Then purchases a cockle-shell, a ballad,†
Or tries to prove fleas lobsters,‡ duckweed salad!
At night he joins the superfine-ear'd crowd,
To hear "The Catalani" scream aloud.
Next morning hurries off with great delight
To see two blackguards, Crib and Belcher, fight:
One day he runs to runs to see a Lord Mayor's show,
The next with dogs and horses—tally-ho!§
A noble lord now mounts the coachman's box,
"Hayt, hayt!" he cries, and on the foot-board knocks:
A *Belcher* round his neck, a *kiddy* smile,
Then capes, topp'd boots, squirts thro' his teeth in style:
Handles the ribands in a natty way;
Proud the stage-coachman's science to display:
Upon the road picks all common slang up,
Which he retails among his "Club of BANG-UP."
A jockey, groom-taught, knowing set of lords,
To whom stage-fighting, *noble* sport affords;
An *upper* order, high bred, titled race,
Who think such *blackguardism* no disgrace.

* A quack, or conjuror, who exhibited his tricks some years ago in Piccadilly, and boasted the wonderful sagacity of a very large black cat in his possession. His placards were always WONDERS.

† The mania for rubbish of this sort has been carried to such a pitch that five pounds have been given at a sale for an old play-bill; antiquity adding such value to useless things! One of the dilletantis, it is said, has expended considerable sums in the purchase of a regular series of turnpike tickets; and another in collecting old ballads, which he has had pasted down in and alphabetical and chronological order.

‡ "Fleas are *not* lobsters, damn their souls." See Pindar's account of Sir Joseph Banks' endeavor to ascertain this important matter.

§ "Our manner of hunting," says Chesterfield, "is only suitable to boobies and bumpkins; the poor beasts are pursued, and run down by much greater beasts than themselves. The true British foxhunter is, most undoubtedly, a species appropriated and peculiar to this country, which no other part of the globe produces."

A bull-bait next delights,* or Cock-lane ghost,†
The last found folly always pleasing most.‡
A monkey-mermaid now he runs to view !§
A "living skeleton's" the next thing new.
Now brother Block comes in with news! Eh, what?
Why, there's a charming Venus-Hottentot!
Pleas'd he starts off, and stares with vacant face,
Then hurries down to join Newmarket Race.
With black-legs there of sweepstakes he converses,
And bets to show his knowledge of race-horses.
"I'll take your bet, my lord, of three to one;
I lay on Slammerkin:" 'tis done and done.
Dup'd of his money, home he steers again,
And to the cockpit hastes to see the *main*.‖

* The amusements of the *Yahoo* a century back (before the intellect began marching) correspond very much with the lion, dog, and stage fighting of the present "enlightened" time. A placard in the time of *Brandy Nan*, announcing bull and bear-baiting at Hockley in the Hole, concludes in the following words: "And a great mad bull will be turned loose in the yard with fireworks all over him, and two or three cats tied to his tail.—Reginat vivat."

† The poor soft cockneys, as well as the *higher orders*, were dreadfully terrified with this hobgoblin for several weeks. The consternation became general; and the great POMPOSO, who was an advocate for every kind of superstitious mummery, gave it full credence. It was also countenanced (no wonder) by all the reverends, and many of the nobility.—See *Walpole's Correspondence*, vol. ii. 333.

‡ "Enchanting novelty, that moon at full,
That finds out every crevice of the head,
That is not sound and perfect, hath in theirs
Wrought this disturbance."—*Cowper*.

§ This humbug served the cockney Yahoos for *pro* and *con*, several months, and even occasioned a lawsuit, being claimed by two owners. It was subsequently discovered to be a composition. A stuffed monkey's skin, to which was attached the tale of a dried fish.

‖ This infernal bloodhound sport is encouraged by Yahoos calling themselves *gentlemen* (Corinthian capitals of polished society). The following advertisement was inserted in the *Morning Post* not long since:—"COCKING.—To be fought at the Royal Cockpit, on Monday, next, and all the week, a great subscription match; begins fighting at half-past six. Dinner on table at four. On Friday morning, in the same week, will be fought a Welsh *main** for £50." Oh, heaven-born Yahoo! Christian and church-goer, no wonder you are compared to angels in your actions!

* This consists in setting 20 or 30 of these poor birds to engage together, armed with steel spurs.—What a picture of hell and demons!

Next night to Drury Lane perhaps he flies,
And praises Master Betty to the skies:
"Oh, what a genius!" he's in rapture lost!
To-morrow he's a dolt—a p——g post.*
But most of all, the Yahoos' chief delight
Is guzzle, whether morning, noon, or night.
That seems their "summum bonum," old or young;
And is their morning, noon, and evening song,
To *that* they fly, to save them from dull thinking,
And such their weakness, that they're proud of drinking.†
For tho' their reason is so much their boast,
Their happiest time is when their reason's lost.
This precious gift the better to display,
They turn the day to night, the night to day.
Witness their midnight Bacchanalian shouts,
And vile, disgusting, swinish, drunken bouts!
Like polecats, stinking with tobacco smoke;
With guzzle drench'd, then comes the song and joke.
Then comes the "tol de rol," and "hey down derry,"
With "push about the glass, and let's be merry."

* The "spread of intellect" was never more conspicuous than at this period. Master Betty's celebrity was wonderful, and the desire to see him perform on the stage so great, that not a place could be secured for the first six nights. The whole town flocked to the theatre to see a parrot-taught boy make love to a woman three or four times his age, big enough to devour him, and who was looking down at him like the cow to Tommy Thumb. The young Roscius, as he was called, was paid for this mummery £50 per night! John Kemble, we are told, was engaged at near £40 per week at the same time. A pretty moderate sum for ranting and bellowing out a few fustian tragedy sentences, larded with ah's and oh's about kings and queens, and such like chinaware.—See *Reynold's Memoirs.*

† "The principle of vanity," says Chesterfield, "is so strong in human nature, that it descends even to the lowest objects. A man will boast, perhaps swear, that he has drunk six or eight bottles of wine at a sitting: out of charity I will believe him a liar, for if I do not I must think him a beast." But there are thousands of popular ballads encouraging this depravity; such as "I guzzle each night till I'm carried up stairs"—"He that goes to bed sober," &c.; or, as Colman observes,

"That there are swilling wights in London town,
Term'd jolly dogs—choice spirits (alias swine)
Who pour, in midnight revels, bumpers down,
Making their throats a thoroughfare for wine."

Broad Grins.

You'll see a score of "reason lords" together,
Smoking the "devil's weed"* in sultry weather!
Stark blind to Chesterfield, and all his graces,†
They puff out clouds in one another's faces:
Each adding to the vile, infernal smother,
As if they meant to stifle one another!
If sulphur was but added to the smell,
It justly might be call'd a little hell.‡
Oh, Jammie, Jammie! what would'st thou have said,
If thou had'st seen a hell like this display'd?
Thy hair, no doubt, would at the horrid sight,
Have push'd thy cap off, and stood bolt upright!
Tho' for a Solomon thou once didst pass,
Thy proper title should be Royal Ass.
To write and rail against the devil's weed,
Proves thee an ass in grain, of long-ear'd breed.

* So called by King James, the first crowned lubber who was dubbed "sacred."

† "Remember the *graces*, for without *them* "ogni fatica e vana."—Adieu: "Les graces, les graces."—*Chesterfield's Letters.*

‡ "Surely smoke becomes a kitchen much better than a dining-chamber, and yet it makes a kitchen oftentimes in the inward parts of men, soiling and infecting them with an unctuous and oily kind of soot, as hath been found in some great tobacco-smokers, that after their death were opened."—*K. James's Counterblast to Tobacco.*

"What a vast traffic is drove, what a variety of labor is performed in the world, to the maintenance of thousands of families, that altother depend on two silly, if not odious customs—the taking of snuff, and smoking of tobacco; both of which, it is certain, do infinitely more harm than good to those who are addicted to them."—*Mandeville's Search into Society.*

"Pass where we may, thro' city or thro' town,
Village or hamlet of this merry land,
Tho' lean and beggar'd, every twentieth pace
Conducts th' unguarded nose to such a whiff
Of stale debauch, forth issuing from the styes
That law has licens'd, as makes temp'rance reel.
There sit involv'd, and lost in curling clouds
Of Indian fume, and guzzling deep, the boor,
The lackey and the groom; the craftsman there
Takes a Lethean leave of all his toil;
Smith, cobbler, joiner, he that plies the shears,
And he that kneads the dough; all loud alike,
All learned, and all drunk."—*Cowper.*

Couldst thou not guess that when thy subjects smoked,
Unless supplied with swill, they'd soon be chok'd?
And that a petty tax upon malt liquor,
Would bring some millions into thy exchequer!*
And millions, all must own, are charming things,
To swell the pockets of poor needy kings.

Nor should the Yahoo's gambling be forgot,
The sure resource of every knave and sot.
Thousands of males and females spend the night,
In shuffling packs of cards—their dear delight!
All sorts, all classes, are engaged in play,
And so deprav'd, they shun the light of day.
'Tis now a master vice, and thrives so well,
That every house is, more or less, a "HELL."
Not for *low* gaming, they scorn *petit jeu*,
'T must be *piquant*, or else it will not do.
Hence Crockford's dashing palaces arise,
To lure rich fools, and dazzle greenhorn's eyes;
Where gudgeons are urged on to make a dash,
By sharks who diddle 'em, and get their cash.

Yes, these are "reason's lords," the strutting race,
Who boast their form divine, and heav'nly grace!
Their faculties perverted, prove their curse,†
And what was bad before, they make still worse.

* The sums produced to the revenue by taxes upon the swill of the Yahoo surpasses belief. With the additional one of tobacco, which appertains as a stimulus to drunkenness, the amount is from ten to twelve millions per annum! No wonder so many sot's holes are seen in every direction.

"The excise is fattened with the rich result
Of all this riot, and ten thousand casks
For ever dribbling out their base contents,
Touch'd by the Midas finger of the state,
Bleed gold for ministers to sport away."—*Cowper.*

† "But when a creature pretending to reason," my master said, "could be guilty of such enormities, he dreaded lest the corruption of that faculty might be worse than brutality itself. He seemed, therefore, confident, that instead of reason, we were only possessed of some quality fitted to increase our natural vices; as the reflection from a troubled stream returns the image of an ill-shapen body, not only *larger*, but more *distorted*."—*Swift.*

To make their own affliction more secure,
Establish laws of primogeniture ;
By which my lord brings up one *cub* in state,
And leaves the rest to curse their ragged fate.
Then, lest Old Nick should envy their condition,
Add to their other curses Superstition !*
The first deprives them of their daily bread,
The latter damns them after they are dead.†
Not all the plagues Pandora's box let out,
Which ever since to curse us, swarm about,
Are half so bad as what these purblind elves,
These "lords of reason" bring upon themselves.‡

Some say the Fates, indeed, like ill-spun toads,
Send us all plagues and troubles by cart-loads.§
That *block* or *hammer* we are doomed to be ;
Thump or be *thump'd* 's our wretched destiny :

* "La superstition," says Helvetius, "est une source empoisonnée, d'où sont sortis tous les malheurs, et les calamités de la terre."

† The heavy curses of primogeniture and superstition stick to the poor Yahoo like a pitch plaster, and keeps his snout to the grindstone to the end of his existence. By the former he is kept, from the extreme inequality of property it occasions, in a state of servitude approaching to slavery and starvation; and by the latter (called religion) rendered an idiot, fed upon moonshine, and cajoled out of the good things in this world, upon an assurance of receiving a hundred fold in another, from a juggling tribe of impostors, who know no more of another world than the beagles they tally-ho with, or the fox they so heroically gallop after, and whose motto ought to be that on the sun-dial—"ignoro quod docěo." The Yahoo, however, in return, is rewarded with the prosing of a "jack in the box" about the wonderful dispensations and goodness of Providence, and gratified with the trumpeters' gaudy laced jackets, with which he ought to be satisfied: and say, as he does over his mutton, "the Lord make us truly thankful."

‡ "Moral evils are of our own making, and undoubtedly the greater part of them may be prevented."—*Southey's Colloquies.*

"I am convinced," says Lord Byron, "that men do more harm to themselves than ever the devil could do to them."

"And feeble suff'rers groan,
With brain-born evils all their own."

§ "And whatsoever we perpetrate,
We do but *row*, we're *steer'd* by Fate."—*Hudibras.*

Predestin'd all to good, or else to evil;
One to Jehovah, fifty to the devil.

What, then, are YAHOOS thus compell'd to be,
The instruments of their own misery ?*
Oh, no ! pride, envy, misery, and ambition,
Have brought " God's image" to this sad condition.
Greedy as death, the universal cry,
Is gold ! more gold ! incessant till they die :
And could they utter words when laid in dust,
More gold ! their livid lips would utter first.
Drain Mexico of gold, bring all Peru ;
Insatiate still, they howl for Timbuctoo.
Gold is the god the Yahoos all adore !
There's no one criminal unless he's poor !
Should Christ himself but visit this proud town,
And ride his ass in Broadway up and down,
The present, though a Bible reading race,
Would shun him, or else giggle in his face :†
While one, perchance, among the happy crowd,
To gratify the rest, might bawl aloud,
(When they had twigg'd him through his glass)
" God damme, Jack, here's Sancho on his ass !
Zounds, what a quizz !"—The belles, too, in a fright,
Would tumble into fits at such a sight.
For pelf they scramble, gold's the grand pursuit,
For gold they'll ransack earth, and hell to boot ;§
Whatever's the pretext, that is still the aim ;
The gen'ral cry is " chacun pour soi-même."

* "Why charge mankind on heaven their own offence,
And call their woes the crimes of Providence?
Blind ; who themselves their miseries create,
And perish by their *folly* not their *fate*."—*Doddsley.*

† "They're now so proud, that should they meet
The twelve apostles in the street,
They'd turn their nose up at them all,
And shove their Savior from the wall."—*Churchill.*

‡ "Hear London's voice—'Get money, money still,
And then let virtue follow if she will:'
Still, still be getting, never, never rest."—*Pope.*

All pull and haul, and kick, and cuff, and grapple,
The worst hog always getting the best apple.

See Sir James Grub, absorb'd in deep-laid schemes,
Gold haunts his thoughts all day, all night his dreams.
Possess'd of half a million, still he's poor,
And saves a penny to increase his store;*
Give him the hide and tallow for his pains,
He'll whip a louse a mile, and boast his gains,
In thrifty maxims he displays his wit,
"Get what you can, and hold fast what you get."
He'll tell you with an oily canting tongue,
"Man wants but little here, and that not long;"†
Tho', from his griping, it appears
As if he thought to live a thousand years.

Did Adam in his garden covet riches?
Why zounds! he wasn't worth a pair of breeches!‡
There were no "*chapeaux-bras*" for Mister Adam,
Nor fringe, nor furbelow,§ to deck his madam!

* "Sir James Lowther, after changing a piece of silver in St. George coffee-house, and paying twopence for his dish of coffee, was helped into his chariot (for he was then very lame and infirm), and proceeded home: a short time after he returned to the house, on purpose to acquaint the woman who kept it that she had given him a bad half-penny, and demanded another in exchange for it. Sir James had about forty thousand pounds per annum, and was at a loss whom to appoint his heir."—*Dr. King's Anecdotes.*

Montaigne observes, "De vray ce n'est pas la disette, c'est plutôt l'abondance qui produit l'avarice."

† The whine of every discontented growling Yahoo, although his factitious wants are gratified every hour in the day, and who requires the two extremes of the globe to be ransacked before he can sit down to his breakfast.

‡ "Time was, when clothing, sumptuous or for use,
Save their own painted skins, our sires had none.
As yet black breeches were not; sath smooth,
Or velvet soft, or plush with shaggy pile."—*Cowper.*

§ According to the old catch, however, the lady was provided with this ornament—

"Adam catch'd Eve by the fur-below;
And that's the oldest catch I know."

It does not seem probable, every thing considered, that Mister Adam

They never dreamed of concerts, balls, or routs,
But wrapp'd their bottoms up in fig-leav'd clouts;*
Till great Jehovah made them skin surtouts,†
That they might look more like their fellow-brutes.

But what's this scramble for? what object's gain'd?
Is real happiness thereby attain'd?
A million may be gain'd by negro gangs,
Who groan beneath church-going Christians' fangs,
Yet bring with it remorse, tho' juggling priests
Say, negroes unbaptized are only beasts;
And pious rum-and-sugar dealing knaves,
Prove from their Bible, "niggers should be slaves;‡
Since Moses says, that Noah (an old Jew)
Got fuddled now and then (as Christians do),

would have spun out his existence to a much longer period (only 930 years) if the *wicked one* had not seduced his rib, nor he have munched the *peepin*, at least if we give credence to the Italian proverb—

"Herba cruda, Donna ignuda,
E dormir a piano terra,
Manda l'uomo sotto terra."

And what else could he boast of in his blessed state?

* In an English Bible (1615) are the following words: "And they sewed up fig leaves together, and made themselves *breeches*."—Genesis iii.—See *Hudibras*.

† "Unto Adam and his wife [did they jump over a broomstick?] did the Lord make coats of skins [what skins?], and clothed them."—Gen. iii. Pretty devils, no doubt, they must have appeared in their bear-skin wrap-rascals! How comes it this precious pair of originals are never represented in our paintings dressed in these eminently beautiful jackets, which they must have undoubtedly been, having been *cut out* by the great Jehovah himself, to whom the *great* Stultz can not be supposed worthy of holding a candle? And is it not greatly to be regretted that the patterns of such magnificent dresses have not been preserved (as the particulars and dimensions of Noah's ark have) for the benefit of the fashionable puppies and their dolls; as they then might have swaggered and strutted "comme il faut," and *rumped* the rabble with a good grace.

‡ "Mr. Canning one day quoted the Bible to sanction Christian slavery, and Mr. Wilberforce had but little to say in reply. And was Christ crucified that black men might be scourged? If so, he had better been born a mulatto, to give both colors an equal chance of freedom, or at least of salvation."—*Byron.*

And in that state was by his son discover'd,
Laying pig fashion,* with his —— uncover'd ;†
Who, grinning like an unlick'd cub, exclaim'd,
"Oh, fie, papa! you ought to be asham'd!
You tipple, and get *pogey* with your wine,
And then lie naked, sprawling like a swine."
But Mister Ham's joke with his Pa—alas!
A *black*-joke prov'd, for lo! "it came to pass,"
That for his graceless prank his generation,
By black skins should betray their degradation :‡
Since when, the woolly-headed, flat-nosed race,
Have been with white-skinn'd Yahoos in disgrace ;§
Who, tho' they flog them, save their precious souls
By baptism, or they'll go to hell in shoals.‖

But let's suppose that Rumpuncheon comes
From negro-driving with a brace of "plums :"
The ill-got wealth but seldom brings content;
For ostentation it is chiefly meant.
His pride, parade, and pomp, and puff, and swell,
And vice and folly, how it's squander'd tell.
Profusion comes with glitter, show, and glare,
And color'd lamps, to make the rabble stare;

* "The little pigs lay with their ...... bare."—*Old Ballad.*

† "And he (Noah) drank of the wine and was drunken, and he was uncovered within his tent. And Ham, the father of Canaan, saw the nakedness of his father."—Gen. ix.

‡ "And Noah awoke from his wine, and knew what his younger son had done unto him." [What had he done?] "And he said, cursed be Canaan, a servant of servants shall he be unto his brethren."—Gen. ix. True Bible justice! the father in fault, and the children all cursed for it.

§ "He finds his fellow guilty of a skin
Not color'd like his own, and having pow'r
T' enforce the wrong, for such a worthy cause,
Dooms and devotes him as his lawful prey."—*Cowper.*

‖ "Happy, thrice happy, now the savage race,
Since Europe takes their *gold* and gives them *grace!*"
Churchill.

While ev'ry thing that's dear or ugly's bought,
And sphinxes, and sarcophaguses sought!*
With costly toys the mansion soon abounds,
The lady's necklace cost ten thousand pounds!†
Baubles of all sorts cram each vacant space,
And dizen'd lacqueys all bedaubed with lace.
Then a grand rout! what exquisite delight
To make a thund'ring through the Square all night!
Three or four hundred fools, or mad folks rather,
To sip slop tea and ices, squeeze together;
Who at the door make such a horrid din,
As if all Bedlam wanted to get in!‡

* "Man's rich with little were his judgment true,
Nature is frugal, and her wants are few;
Those few wants answered, bring sincere delights;
But fools create themselves new appetites:
Fancy and pride seek things at vast expense,
Which relish not to reason or to sense."—*Young.*

"Hunger, thirst, and nakedness, are the first tyrants that force us to stir; afterward our pride and sloth, sensuality and fickleness, are the great patrons that promote all arts and sciences, trades and callings." —*Mandeville's Search into Society.*

† Who could suppose that such an enormous sum could ever be demanded for a string of baubles, to hang round the neck of a female Yahoo? It is however certain that a necklace of that estimated value was purloined, a few years since, from the shop of Messrs. Rundle & Bridge, and a great reward offered for the recovery. Yet £10,000 at the present day seems nothing, since within the last year or two we have heard a trinket of the same sort, belonging to the Princess of Orange, was *filched* ("conveyed," the wise call it,) at Brussels, worth *only* £80,000. *Goramity* has blessed the Yahoo with *wisdom* to some purpose!

Voltaire supposes the two hundred snippings, called foreskins, which *holy* David, like a gallant suitor, brought King Saul, were strung on a pack-thread, and intended for a necklace for the fair Miss Michal, his daughter. The Lord's anointed (her daddy) had indeed only demanded *one* hundred as the price of the lady; but David generously brings double the number required, unwilling she should be deficient in such precious nicknacks for the ornament of her person, or toilette.

‡ It is a part of the etiquette of these moon-stricken assemblages to make as much noise as possible with the knocker at the street-door, which is rattled with all the fury of a frenzied lunatic for about half a minute upon the arrival of every carriage; and if three or four parties arrive at the same time, they are let in separately, the door shut, and the horrible thundering at the knocker repeated by each, by which the

Now crowding, pushing, treading on a corn;
And shawls, and scarfs, and gauze, and muslins torn:
While screw'd-up dolls and dandies, daub'd with paint,
Have all their laces cut, or else they faint.*
And then what pleasure next day to peruse,
A puff'd-up, paid-for statement in the News!
"Lady Rumpuncheon's rout, and grand display†
Of all the rank and fashion of the day.
With all the delicacies of the season"
(The puffer knows what sort of cant is pleasing).‡
Viola high life! the ton among the great!
The folks possessing "plums," who live in state!
What "march of mind!" for an enlighten'd nation!
What cagmag stuff for "lords of the creation!"§

uproarious din is continued for hours together, to the great delight of the neighbors, who are all tarred with the same stick, and highly amused with this "hell broke loose" racket. To heighten the absurdity, the rout-givers send their empty carriages round the next morning, with a footman, and cards of compliments, and inquiry after the welfare of the parties who honored their "little St. Luke's" the preceding evening! Oh, what happiness to exist in such a *truly* enlightened age!—See *Don Juan*, canto ix., stanza 67.

* The lacing up these be-whiskered, cigar-smoking puppies, is a modern refinement in dress, supposed to contribute to the *elegance* of the Yahoo's shape (pretty dears!) and is an indubitable proof of the so much boasted march of intellect. That *she* dolls, who are milliners, or priest-governed from the cradle to the coffin, should give way to such silliness is not to be wondered at—but, for great long-legged, brawny-backed lubbers to affect such molly-coddle, contemptible effeminacy, is most disgraceful!

"Fops at all corners, lady-like in mien,
Civetted puppies, smelt ere they are seen."—*Trocinium.*

† "This lady glories in profuse expense,
And thinks *distraction* is magnificence."—*Young.*

‡ See this contemptible sort of puffing happily ridiculed in a burlesque expose of a Blowbladder street rout in Bulliana.

§ "But the long pomp, the midnight masquerade,
With all the freaks of wanton wealth array'd;
In these ere triflers half their wish obtain,
The toiling pleasure sickens into pain;
And e'en while fashion's brightest arts decoy,
The heart distrusting, asks if this be joy?"—*Goldsmith.*

By loyalty and highborn blockheads bred*
(When a fish stinks, 'tis first about the head),
Descending then to cits and plebs it goes,
And over all the tide of folly flows,†
Reaching at last the "multitude of swine,"
Who in *their* turn have routs! and stink and shine.‡

Such is the blessed Christian Yahoo race,
Who, whitewashed in *lamb's* blood, abound in grace:
Such is the saint-like crew, who talk of heaven,
Tho' all infected with the devil's leaven.
A gospel-poring, canting tribe, who boast
Of fellowship (God bless us) with a ghost!§
A sacramental, pure, craw-thumping herd,
All saved by faith, thro' Jesus Christ their Lord:
Who lie, and trick, and cozen all the week,‖
And on the Lord's day go the Lord to seek.

* See *Don Juan* canto x., stanza 85. "Oh, Mrs. Fry!"

† "But, lo! the fatal victor of mankind,
Swoll'n *luxury!*—pale ruin stalks behind!"—*Essay on Satire.*

‡ "Increase of power begets increase of wealth;
Wealth luxury, and luxury excess;
Excess, the scrofulas and itchy plague,
That seizes first the opulent, descends
To the next rank contagious, and in time
Taints downward all the graduated scale
Of order from the chariot to the plough."—*Cowper.*

§ "And the fellowship of the Holy Ghost be with you all evermore."—*Liturgy.*

‖ "Two gods divide them all—pleasure and gain:
For these they live. Lust in their hearts
And mischief in their hands, they roam the earth
To prey upon each other."—*Cowper.*

It is not long since one of the petty African kings said, "he would send his son to England, to learn to read book, and be great rogue." This negro had formed no incorrect opinion of the civilization which he had seen, and of the *education* which is given in the *school of trade!* —*Southey's Colloquies.*

"When you have seen a little of the world," says Sir Walter Scott, "you will then be no stranger to the policy of life, which deals in mining and countermining." The *real* opinion the Yahoos entertain of one another is pretty evidently shown by their always requiring *stamped* receipts in their respective payments. Why demand *legal*

At church, and tell him in a whining tone,
That they have *done things* they should *not* have done.*
(All which he knew before, but that's no matter,
He's pester'd weekly with their pious patter),†
Inform him, in their silly, gabbling way,
That they have, like lost muttons, gone astray.
("Muttons!" Jehovah cries, when this he hears,
"Od rabbit 'em, they're asses, wolves, and bears.")
Invoke the Lamb, "*that* takes away their sins,"‡
Beg for dry bread, but long for greasy chins,
(As if the Lord had nothing else to do
But bake them bread!—they'll ask him next to brew!
And add by way of *rider* to their pray'r,
That he will please to send them better fare).§
Told by the parson whatsoe'er they want,
If ask'd devoutly for, the Lord will grant,‖
And thus encourag d, such bold-fac'd humgruffins
May next beg tea, and toast, and butter'd muffins!

binding while they have such high opinions of each other's integrity and principles? Is not this indubitable proof, notwithstanding the blarney they so liberally bestow upon one another, that they can not be trusted? Swift says in a letter to Dr. Sheridan, "You should think every man a rogue, but not tell him so."

* The *doing of things*, and leaving of things *undone*, form part of the so much admired liturgy, which is held up, by the craft, as the finest and most sublime composition that was ever given to a benighted world for the edification of enlightened Yahoos.

† One should suppose the great Jehovah, every Sunday morning, when he awoke, and recollected the day, would call to Gabriel to keep the doors and shutters close, that he might not be bored with the horrible din of the Christian Yahoos about the carpenter's son and the Ghost. Or say, as Quin used to his man, on very gloomy mornings, "Call me to-morrow, John."

‡ "Oh, Lamb of God, *that* takest away the sins of the world."—*Liturgy.*

§ A little boy, who scarcely ever tasted any thing but dry bread and potatoes, repeating his prayers one day, said, "Mammy, mayn't I ask *Godamighty* for a little bit of cheese to-day?"

‖ "And dost promise that when two or three are gathered together in thy name, thou wilt grant their requests." Why, then, do these gulls flock in such crowds to their slop-shops, and at such an expense and loss of time, when they could have whatever they wished for by a little gossiping assemblage in the name of the Lord at home?

Or (heedless of the great Jehovah's trouble),
Request some day a dish of *squeak and bubble!*

Oh, great Jehovah! how art thou beset,
Do not these Yahoos put thee in a sweat?
No wonder thou shouldst grieve for having made 'em,*
They've plagued thee ever since the days of Adam.
Tho' in a horse-pond thou hast soused one litter,
The present brood seem very little better.
Couldst thou not from thy prescience see at first,
They'd turn out rubbish, being made of dust?†
Provok'd to wrath, how often hast thou swore‡
That they should never enter thy street door.
When did they ever heed thy oaths or threats?
Not even while they were thy darling pets:
And shouldst thou send down stairs again a Ghost,
With Chip to mend 'em, 'twould be labor lost.
Their actions show that Nick's their sov'reign lord;
They neither mind thee, nor thy holy word.
Hadst thou not twice the patience of poor Job,
Thou'dst doff thy golden crown and day-light robe,§
Slip on thy thick-soled shoes, and come and kick 'em,
Or send the angel Gaby down to *lick* 'em;
A good sound drubbing for such mumping scrubs,
Might chance to cure them of the mulligrubs.
But if they should not mend by kicks and thumps,
Clap Lord Monboddo's tail upon their rumps;‖
They'd then be (tails would so improve the breed)
The "paragon of animals" indeed.—

* "And it repented the Lord that he had made man on the earth, and it grieved him at his heart."—Genesis vi.

† "And the Lord God formed man of the dust of the ground."—Genesis ii.

‡ "Unto whom I sware in my wrath that they should not enter into my rest."—Psalm xcv.

§ "With light as a robe,
Thou hast thyself clad."—Psalm civ.

‖ "Lord Monboddo supposed the human race were originally furnished with tails, which have been worn away by their sitting so much upon them."

Such strutting, puff'd-up, self-conceited buzzards,
Fasting, or full, still grumbling in their gizzards;
Such squabby, tadpole, gut-and-garbage creatures!
Some (tho' all boast their angel form and features!)
With such rotundity of paunch and bottom,
They'll make the devil jack-weights, when he's got 'em:*
With precious souls, tag, rag, and bobtail cramm'd;
Exulting at the risk of being damn'd!†
Such bloated buffos, boasting immortality,
Without an atom's weight of rationality.
Search thro' the universe you'll never trace
A more ridiculous or vicious race.
Whatever other planets may possess
Of living animals, we're left to guess;
But none in fifty worlds you'd ever find,
Who were to vice and folly more inclin'd.‡
And if to Paradise the Yahoos go,
And I were ask'd to enter, I'd cry No:
Like the poor negro, who when tortur'd said,§
"Massa, you go to 'ebben when you dead?"

* Would not the massive members of the church (as Lord Byron styles them), as well as Alderman Paunch, Lord Gundygut, Lady Foulfirkin, and some others of high degree, answer very well for this purpose, and turn the Devil's meat-spits round merrily if they were tied neck and heels together?

† "So excessive is human vanity," says Lord Bolingbroke, "that although it is admitted that nine out of ten are damned, yet immortality is the boast, and the risk of hell-fire disregarded."

‡ "——— where to rampant vigor grown,
Vice chokes up every virtue, where, self-sown,
The seeds of folly shoot forth rank and bold,
And every seed brings forth a hundred fold."—*Churchill.*

§ The tortures inflicted on these poor creatures, as well as on the Caribs and Maroons, the aborigines of the West India Islands, exceed all credibility, and chill the blood by a recital; but Christians, with the Bible in their hands, are self-justified in committing the most horrible barbarities: they are serving the Lord by smiting the heathens, which covers and authorizes every species of wickedness and cruelty, and stifles every feeling of humanity. Smollett, speaking of an insurrection of the negro slaves of Jamaica, in the year 1760, says, "After they were subdued, they were put to death by a variety of tortures. Some were hanged, some beheaded, some burned, and some fixed alive upon gibbets. One of these last lived eight days and eighteen hours,

" Yes, you black dog, I shall."—" Oh, very well,"
Poor Sambo cries, " den me go lib in hell."*

CONCLUSION.

Now, who to patients in this curst condition,
Would ever be adviser or physician?
In their derang'd *obnoodle*-headed state,†
Try but to cure them—your reward's their hate.
Like pigs that in a dirty puddle lie,
They take delight to wallow in their sty;
And he who tries to pull them out will get,
As Æsop's gard'ner did, his fingers bit.‡

suspended under a vertical sun, without being refreshed by one drop of water, or receiving any manner of sustenance. Numbers of these poor creatures escaped to the mountains and woods, and killed themselves in despair."—*History of England*, vol. v., p. 160. Oh, blessed and holy Christian slave-drivers! well, are ye entitled to a place in Abraham's bosom! "Preachee and floggee," that's your sort. There's a Christian parson always ready to absolve ye: nothing's required but *faith* in your *blessed Redeemer*.

* "In vain you talk to them of shades below,
They fear no hell but where the Christians go."—*De Foe.*

† *Obnoodle-headed!* Impossible! What! so wise a race as the Yahoos? who were 2,000 years in finding out the right way to turn the handle of a spoon. It should be *obnubilated*, no doubt—the Rhinoceros, as he was cognominated (to use his own expression) by Tom Davis, would, excepting when he wished to express himself in *curt*,* have adopted obnubilated, offuscated, obumbrated, or some long-tailed sesquipedale to denote stupidity. The great doctor's bombast was never more happily ridiculed than by Peter Pindar, who says he gives

"A pyramid's importance to a pin;
On ev'ry theme alike his pompous art,
The gen'ral conflagration, or a. . . ."—*Benev. Epistle.*

‡ "Now he's a fool who never thinks
Of meddling with an ass:

* The doctor's own slang.

Religion's frenzy has, 'tis very plain,
Contaminated every Yahoo's brain.*
Are Chesterfield's incurables† now mended?
Oh, no! his hospital is much extended.
The world is one huge Bedlam, there's no doubt,
A few call'd *inside* patients—millions *out*.‡
Blackmore affirmed that all mankind were mad,§
Some slightly so, some worse, some very bad.
And as in ev'ry class, and ev'ry station,
There's what pig Johnson‖ calls concatenation,

The more you stir, the more its stinks,
In every dirty case."—*Tim Bobbin.*

"Society," says the Laureat (before he smelt the sack), "may, with great propriety, be compared to an ass that kicks those who attempt to relieve it of its burden."—*Letters from Spain.*

And the same tune sings the *New Monthly Magazine.*

"With priests rant and rave about sin,
With Nick's kitchen underground frighten;
With mountebanks make the mob grin,
Do every thing but enlighten.
He that aims at enlightening only out doles
An ophthalmic drug to a nation of moles."

* "The history of Christians and of Christianity is altogether, and without exception, a history of madmen and lunacy."—*Perry's Defence.*

† The "Hospital of Incurables," was Lord Chesterfield's classical and appropriate denomination of the Corinthian capitals, alias the House of Lords.

"If you knew what a hopeless and lethargic den of dullness and drawling our *hospital* is during a debate, and what a mass of corruption in its patients, you would wonder not that I very seldom speak, but that I ever attempted it."—*Lord Byron and his Contemporaries.*

‡ "Our world," says Lord Bolingbroke, "seems to be, in many respects, the Bedlam of every other system of intelligent creatures." —*Philosophical Essays.* Of which opinion is also Voltaire. "Le monde est un grand Bedlam où des Fous enchaînent d'autres Fous." —*Pot Pourri.*

Erasmus hardly excepts any. "Presque tous les hommes," he observes, "sont Fous: (a quoi bon ce *presque?* il n'y a pas un seul homme qui n'extravague de plus d'une manière:) ils sont donc tous semblables en ce point là."—*Erasme sur la Folie.*

§ See Sir Richard Blackmore on the Spleen.

‖ "Why, I pray you, is not the pig, and the great, and the huge, all one."—*Fluellin.*

Connected by some circumstance or other,
There's no Mad Tom but soon he finds a brother.

Well—since the whole's a mass of half-craz'd things,
Lords, beggars, fools, pickpockets, priests, nnd kings,
With nondescripts of all sorts out of number,
We'll class them altogether as live lumber,
And recommend it as the *wisest* thing,
That they should play the *fool*, and dance and sing;
And tho' with hell-fire threatened, if they frisk it,
Defy Black Jack, and all his imps, and risk it;
But if, while they were capering and leaping,*
The old grim rascal should by chance be peeping;
Provided with a good strong casting-net,
What a choice draught of Yahoos he would get!
Exulting, no doubt, Blackey then would bawl,
"Odd zounds and blood! but here's a glorious haul!
Except in war time I but seldom catch
So many of these shabrags at a batch.

* Messrs. Beelzebub and Co. are commissioned by the saints to lay violent hands on all the capering tribe whenever they can catch them. Saint Augustin, a saint of the first class, consigns all such wicked sinners over to the Old One, *sans ceremonie.* "The miserable dancer," exclaims the ranting Bedlamite, "knows not that as many paces as he maketh in dancing, so many *leaps* he maketh in hell." Another of these holy twattlers, Jerome, a saint also of great renown, tells us that "the very touch of a wanton is worse than the bite of a mad dog." And does not the great saint of saints, Paul, the head of the gang, and favorite spouter of the godly snufflers, tell us, that "it is good for a man not to touch a woman."—1 Cor. vii. No wonder the petticoat tribes are all so priest-ridden, and dangle so after the parsons everywhere, to whom they always seem ready to lie down before they are asked even to sit. A ranting evangelical, preaching upon the text, "It is good for a man not to touch a woman," concluded by saying, "And now, my beloved, let me remind you of the sin of incontinence, which will lead you to destruction. Satan's most powerful arms are women; do not damn yourselves for such silly things. Beware of the *bottomless* pit. Recollect the apostle's advice, and touch not a woman."

"All flesh is grass," 'tis very true, alas!
But then a woman's flesh is scurvy grass!

One might suppose that I had risen to-day,
Like Madame Plump, a . . e upward as they say.*
Poor Yahoos! aye, aye, ye may well look glum,
You're holy water sprinkling's all a *hum.*
No forty-parson power can set you free,
You're Lamb and Pigeon won't bamboozle me;
If you think fudge-like that can save your bacon,
You're Johnny-raws, and damnably mistaken;
To my den under ground you all must go,
And shake your trotters in the shades below;†
Where, since you're all to capering so inclined,
Both choice and cheap you'll cat-gut scrapers find.
Allons donc, ragamuffins! scamper, trot,
Perhaps you'll find my kitchen rather hot;
But pluck up courage, you'll have neighbors' fare,
You'll meet with millions of your *comrogues* there;
For tho' ye're pupp'd with an immortal soul,
Nineteen in twenty come to my dark hole;‡

* *Lady Answerall.*—"Well, she had good luck to draw Tom Plump into wedlock—she ris with her a..e upward."

Miss Neverout.—"Fie, madam! what do you mean?"

Lady Smart.—"O, Miss! 'tis nothing what we say among ourselves."
Polite Conversation.

† Since the Devil is allowed by Milton to crack his jokes when his cannon-balls are knocking the angels one over the other like ninepins, he may fairly be allowed a little jocularity on the present occasion, when he has nabbed so many of the Yahoos by a coup-de-maître.

"———————— down they fell
By thousands, angel on archangel roll'd.
———————— Satan beheld their plight,
And to his notes thus in derision called—
Oh, friends, why come not on these victors proud?
Ere while the fierce were coming—
——————— straight they chang'd their minds,
Flew off, and into strange vagaries fell,
As they would dance; yet for a dance they seem'd
Somewhat extravagant and wild."—*Paradise Lost.*

‡ "Christians do virtually attribute to the Devil an empire much more extensive than that of the Supreme Being. The latter with difficulty saves a few *elect*, while the former carries off in spite of him the greater part of mankind, who listen to his destructive temptations rather than to the absolute commands of God."—*Christianity Unveiled*

Your 'godlike' qualities, so much your boast,
Are 'all my eye,' when here ye come to roast.
Jehovah's made ye, any one may see,
Not for himself; oh, no, ye're made for me."*

The sooty rascal, then, perhaps, might take
His passage home across the "level lake,"
And landing with his cargo safe and sound,
Shoot 'em all in his cellar, underground;
While all his imps would come in troops and sing,
Long life to Beelzebub, their noble king!

* From the immense and countless number of Yahoos' souls (whatever they may be made of) that are daily and hourly arriving with passports for the devil's territories, he is certainly justified in making this assertion, and exulting over the poor lost muttons. The black gentleman, no doubt, reads the holy book sometimes, "pour s'amuser," and there finds his boundaries are to be enlarged,* from which he naturally will draw the above inference, and look for his subjects twenty or thirty abreast; and not "en file" through Sambo's "narrow paff," which he told his brodder niggers, "leadeff to ebbenly moosic, and ebbery ting dem like."

* "Therefore, hell hath enlarged herself, and opened her mouth without measure."—Isaiah v.

THE END.

THE YAHOO! a Satirical Rhapsody. By the author of the Great Dragon Cast Out. "The Yahoo is very witty and clever. The satire is broad, and carries humor farther even than Dean Swift carried it. Its cuts at public men are very clever; and the author is certainly not a friend to clerical aggressions."—*Sunday London Despatch.*

www.ingramcontent.com/pod-product-compliance
Lightning Source LLC
LaVergne TN
LVHW021424110826
845150LV00007B/2074

* 9 7 8 1 4 2 5 5 0 8 0 5 0 *